D0025267

# EDUCATION
# OF THE
# BLACK ADULT
# IN THE
# UNITED STATES

# EDUCATION OF THE BLACK ADULT IN THE UNITED STATES

## An Annotated Bibliography

*Compiled by*
LEO McGEE *and* HARVEY G. NEUFELDT

Bibliographies and Indexes in Afro-American and African Studies, Number 4

GREENWOOD PRESS
Westport, Connecticut • London, England

*374*
*McGee*

**Library of Congress Cataloging in Publication Data**

McGee, Leo.
    Education of the Black adult in the United States.

    (Bibliographies and indexes in Afro-American and
African studies, ISSN 0742-6925 ; no. 4)
    Bibliography: p.
    Includes indexes.
    1. Afro-Americans—Education—United States—History.
2. Adult education—United States—History.  3. Afro-
Americans—Vocational education—United States—History.
I. Neufeldt, Harvey G.  II. Title.  III. Series.
LC2801.M27   1985      374′.008996073      84-19785
ISBN 0-313-23473-6 (lib. bdg.)

Copyright © 1985 by Leo McGee and Harvey G. Neufeldt

All rights reserved. No portion of this book may be reproduced, by any
process or technique, without the express written consent of the publisher.

Library of Congress Catalog Card Number: 84-19785

ISBN: 0-313-23473-6
ISSN: 0742-6925

First published in 1985

Greenwood Press
A division of Congressional Information Service, Inc.
88 Post Road West, Westport, Connecticut 06881

Printed in the United States of America

10 9 8 7 6 5 4 3 2 1

Dedicated to the millions of African descent
who were unrelenting in their quest for intellectual growth

# CONTENTS

# INTRODUCTION

Until very recently the term "Adult Education" had little meaning to educators and laymen alike. This lack of understanding prevailed despite the operation of numerous educational programs for adults and the multiplicity of scholarly pursuits of adult education academicians. The field of adult education is relatively new when compared with other major disciplines. In the general sense it has been going on since the beginning of time, but its major strides toward becoming a well-defined field of study have come about in the twentieth century--primarily since 1920.

Among the forerunners in establishing academic programs in this field are Columbia, Ohio State, Chicago and Florida State universities. Today the number of available programs are multiplied greatly. These programs are primarily designed to give students an understanding of adult learning, adult psychology, process of aging and administration of education programs for adults.

There is no universally accepted definition of adult education. Occasional synonymous terms such as career education, vocational education and continuing education increase the complexities of this dilemma. Most scholars in the field accept the definition offered by Cyril Houle:

> Adult education is the process by which men and women (alone, in groups, or in the institutional settings) seek to improve themselves or their society by increasing their skill, their knowledge, or their sensitiveness. Any process by which individuals, groups or institutions try to help men and women improve in these ways.

In accordance with this definition, blacks have engaged in adult education since their arrival in this country. Throughout history, efforts by black adults to obtain an education has necessitated a struggle. From the time they were forced on the American scene to the present, their education has been at an absolute premium. When slaves first entered the new world they had to become educated for sheer survival and to carry out their labor assignments.

Early advocates of education for blacks can be placed in four categories:  first, plantation owners who recognized the economic benefit of skilled slaves; second, persons in sympathy with the oppressed; third, missionaries who believed that God's grace was for all; fourth, ambitious blacks who aspired to a better life.

Throughout the Colonial period questions were raised regarding the status of blacks.  The Christian theory created one of the greatest moral dilemmas in American history.  It suggested that all men were created equal in the sight of God.  This brought about a great sense of guilt among merchants and plantation  owners who were advocates of Christianity and yet desired to continue their lucrative profit from the slave trade and slave labor.  Most continued to advocate Christianity while at the same time endorsing slavery.

Blacks did not receive "formal" education during the Colonial period. No legislation was enacted for this purpose.  However, many did receive training in an informal way from religious groups, plantation families and by other clandestine means.

Black adults engaged in their first systematic educational experience on the plantation.  On-the-job training programs were established to train slaves for special skills.  Training slaves became profitable business in that it improved the economic efficiency of the plantation and produced a cadre of highly marketable slaves.  Many carpenters, blacksmiths, weavers, tailors, cobblers, wheelwrights, masons, barbers and seamstresses were prepared as a result of this instruction.  Numerous plantations became self-sustaining due to the food, clothing, tools and houses produced by slave labor.

This type of apprenticeship training for selected slaves was instituted on nearly all plantations.  Those plantations that did not have their own training programs were able to benefit from others through the availability of trained slaves at auctions and the possibilities of having slaves sent out for training.

This training system began to deteriorate at the beginning of the Civil War.  However, the Union Army functioned as a school for the enlisted black soldiers and the adult civilians that flocked behind Union lines.  Schooling that black adults received was, in general, the result of Army officers and their wives and chaplains.

The black convention and black press movement was set in motion prior to the Civil War.  Devoted to mass education of their people, convention leaders used several educational methods to reach the black community including debates, public lectures, group discussions and petitions to state legislatures and Congress.  These instructional strategies enhanced public awareness and understanding of issues involving the oppressed.  The black press was an important factor in bringing leaders together and in disseminating information about these meetings.

From the outset, there was a great deal of interdependency between black conventions and the black press.  Their work was inextricably interwined.  It was through the press that many of the issues of the day reached the black masses, while the press looked to the conventions for its most newsworthy materials. The primary goal of both was the education of black people. At times, the actions of these entities were considered revolutionary by many whites bent on keeping blacks in their place. The major issues addressed usually centered around politics, civil rights and education which were perceived by black adults as pivotal points for shaking the shackles of slavery.

The significance of local, state, regional and national black conventions in the development of American thought, in many ways, has been overlooked. The convention movement began around 1830 and extended through the late 1890's. Black leaders of that period were the staunchest supporters of the conventions, many of whom were associated with black newspapers. The conventions provided a forum in large Northern urban centers where competition for jobs became intense. This seemed to increase prejudices against blacks in the North, particularly around the mid-1870's.

Secondly, the denial of black expression was another significant reason for the establishment of separate conventions. With the number of free blacks increasing from 59,000 in 1790 to 319,000 in 1830, a means of conveying grievances in a united front to the American society was deemed a necessity.

Seeking a safeguard from further enslavement was the third reason for black convention advocacy. Education was considered to be a preventive measure. It was felt that an enlightened people would be less likely to permit themselves to be subjected to mental or physical abuses, inequities or inhumanity.

While there were many thousands of whites from the North as well as the South who were helpful in the education of blacks, there were many blacks who made noteworthy contributions to the education of the black adult, three of which merit special mention. Booker T. Washington and George Washington Carver as a team at Tuskegee Institute did much for black adults. They conducted many practical programs and demonstration projects for black farmers throughout Alabama. Although preaching the gospel of accommodation, they had a positive influence on their constituents' outlook toward education.

Dr. Alain Locke was the third black contributor. He was an eminent scholar who distinguished himself as an academic adult educator. He was particularly effective in articulating the educational problems and concerns of black adults during the early 1900's.

Around the second decade of the twentieth century organized educational programs for adults began to materialize. Services offered by many were available to blacks. The Cooperative Extension Service began the array of programs and was followed by programs sponsored by the Jeans, Rosenwald and Carnegie funds, the Federal Emergency Relief Administration (FERA), the Work Progress Administration (WPA), Civilian Conservation Corps (CCC), Manpower Development Training Act (MDTA), Adult Basic Education (ABE) and Comprehensive Employment Training Act (CETA). These programs in their individual ways have influenced the lives of millions of black American adults.

"Education of Black Adults" is a component of American History that
has been largely overlooked by historians.  Literature on this subject
is more obscure than on the general subject of black education.  What is
necessary today is to view American education in a more comprehensive
manner than in the past and to bring about a greater understanding of
the educational plight of blacks in this country.  This book focuses on
the efforts put forth over a three-century period to educate the black
adult.  It contains over three hundred annotated sources that address
the subject of black adult education.  It is divided into four
periods—Pre-Civil War, Civil War, Separate but Equal, and Modern Era.

Pre-Civil War (1619-1860):  The Quakers took the lead in educating
blacks during the Colonial period.  Instruction was mainly of a
religious nature.  A number of day and evening schools were established
for blacks which opened their doors to the young and the old.

Education through apprenticeship was also significant during this
period.  Thousands of black artisans were produced as a result of this
system of training.

Civil War and Reconstruction (1860-1880):  The first concerted
attempt to reduce illiteracy among the black masses took place in the
South during this period.  The Union Army became a type of school for
the enlisted black soldiers and others who took refuge behind its lines.
The Federal Government enacted legislation which created the Freedmen's
Bureau.  This organization, established to assist in the affairs of the
freedmen, made education one of its major thrusts.  In addition,
missionary organizations were prominent throughout this period.  They
were instrumental in the establishment of schools and educational
programs for blacks throughout the South.

Two major questions received considerable debate during this period:
Should blacks be educated?  If blacks should be educated, what should
be the nature of their education?

Separate But Equal (1880-1930):  The general consensus was that
blacks should be educated.  What type and how much remained unanswered.
There were no easy answers to these questions in that they were pondered
by a society that defined blacks as separate and subordinate.

This period witnessed a gradual withdrawal of the Federal Government
from the realm of black education and black rights.  "Separate but
Equal" undergirded the system of education across the South.

Modern Era (1930-present):  During this period there was a return of
Federal support of black education.  Many of the Federally sponsored
educational programs launched under President Franklin D. Roosevelt's
administration benefited blacks.  Some of the most noted Federal
programs throughout this period include Cooperative Extension Service,
Tennessee Valley Authority, Work Progress Administration, Civilian
Conservation Corps, Manpower Development Act, Comprehensive Employment
Training Act and Adult Basic Education.

A small number of the resources overlap the periods identified in
this publication.  They are titled General Resources.

This is the first comprehensive annotated bibliography on the subject of black adult education. It is a resource that should be useful at the university, school system and community level.

# 1
# PRE–CIVIL WAR, 1619–1860

1. Bell, Howard H. "The American Moral Reform Society, 1836-1841."
Journal of Negro Education, 27:34-40 (Winter, 1958).

Bell describes and analyzes the rise, goals and demise of the
American Moral Reform Society under the leadership of James Forten.
The importance of the American Moral Reform Society for the black
adult lay in its emphasis upon education, temperance, economic
advancement and universal liberty and in its call to the black
churches to attack slavery.

2. _____. "Free Negroes of the North 1830-1835: A study in
National Cooperation." Journal of Negro Education, 26:447-455 (Fall,
1957).

Bell provides a description of the cooperative efforts of Northern
blacks in organizing conventions designed to promote education,
economic improvement and self-help. Examples included the National
Convention, the Colored American Conventional Temperance Society and
the Moral Reform Society. All in all, the convention movement
played an important role in the education of the free black
community prior to the Civil War.

3. _____. "A Survey of the Negro Convention Movement, 1830-
1861." Ph.D. dissertation, Northwestern University, 1953.

The Negro convention movement was a valuable tool for educating the
black masses on specific subjects such as infidelism, Christianity,
slavery, justice, suffrage, temperance, education and moral reform.
The movement reached its peak during the years preceeding the Civil
War. Convention leaders and delegates made their ideas known by
debating on the assembly floor, drawing up resolutions, making
public addresses and framing petitions.

There were eleven national conventions held between 1830 and 1861;
however, there were many times that number held at the state level.

This dissertation discusses in detail many of the conventions held during this period.

4.  Bellamy, Donnie D.  "The Education of Blacks in Missouri Prior to 1861."  Journal of Negro History, 59:143-157 (April, 1974).

Although the article focuses primarily on the education of black children in Missouri, mention is also made of the importance of Sunday Schools in the education of black adults in Missouri in the nineteenth century.  Of special importance in this article is the discussion of the Roman Catholic Church's contribution in establishing both day and night schools for blacks.

5.  Berlin, Ira.  "Slaves Who Were Free:  The Free Negro in the Upper South, 1776-1861."  Ph.D. dissertation, University of Wisconsin, 1970.

The author contends that "Most American free Negroes lived neither in the North nor in the fabled Negro quarters of the Gulf Coast Cities.  In fact, the majority of American freedmen and the overwhelming majority of Southern freedmen lived in the Upper South-- Delaware, Maryland, Virginia, Kentucky, Missouri, North Carolina and Tennessee.  Baltimore, not New Orleans, New York or even Philadelphia, had the largest urban black population."

The study describes the life of the free Negroes:  how they lived, worked, married, raised families, educated, entertained, improved and protected themselves.

6.  _____.  Slaves Without Masters.  New York:  Pantheon Books, 1974.

This book is about the free Negro in the South prior to Emancipation. "They were slaves without masters."  Many were able to acquire wealth and social standing.  "A few masterless slaves, themselves, became slave masters."

Although many writers contend that in the eyes of whites the lives of free Negroes were not much different from that of the slaves, Berlin points out that the free Negro did experience a much higher quality of life.  The freedom he enjoyed permitted him to progress educationally.  Day and evening schools in the North were established for children as well as adults.

7.  Blassingame,  John W.  The Slave Community:  Plantation Life in the Antebellum South.  New York:  Oxford University Press, 1972.

Blassingame has provided an excellent analysis of the acculturation process within the slave community.  Focusing heavily on auto- biographies of blacks and supplemented by autobiographies of whites, plantation records, agricultural journals and travel accounts, Blassingame has explored not so much what the whites sought to teach the slaves but rather what blacks learned within the slave quarters. Highlighted are the importance of music, religion, folk tales, the dance and funeral rites in the slaves' attempts to preserve their culture.

Blassingame rejects the assumption that slaves were totally stripped of their African heritage.  Instead, he argues that the slaves were able to maintain some remnants of their culture and thereby gain a sense of worth and a degree of freedom both in thought and action.

Blassingame has provided an excellent case study of education, including adult education, in the broad or informal sense.  He has clearly demonstrated that what is learned or appropriated by a community is not necessarily what was intended by those in power, in this case, by the white slave owners and clergymen.

8.  Boskin, Joseph.  "The Origins of American Slavery:  Education as an Index of Early Differentiation."  Journal of Negro Education, 35:125-133 (Spring, 1966).

This article affirms that a small portion of the Negro population did receive religious and secular training during the Colonial period, mainly in haphazard fashion.

9.  Brigham, R. I.  "Negro Education in Antebellum Missouri."  Journal of Negro History, 30:405-420 (October, 1945).

Using the case study of a Missouri slave, Brigham describes and analyzes the opportunity of Missouri slaves to learn not only a trade but also to gain a rudimentary knowledge of reading and writing.  The state law of 1847 which forbad anyone to keep school for or to teach Negroes limited the impact of Sunday Schools and day schools for Missouri blacks.  Consequently, most slaves learned from their environment rather than in schools.  Brigham's case study focuses primarily on the educational experience of those slaves who were "hired out."  What is not clear, however, is the extent to which the experiences of the "hired out" slaves were the exception rather than the norm for the slave community.

10.  Bruce, Phillip A.  The Plantation Negro as a Freedman.  New York: Putnam's Sons, 1889.

One of the early publications dealing with the plantation Negro, this study highlights the domination of the skilled trades by Negroes prior to emancipation.  Bruce argues that technical jobs on the plantation were handled by slaves and apprenticeship training was handled by Negro journeymen.  A key chapter relevant for the study of the education of the black adult is Chapter 15 entitled "Mechanics."

Skilled slaves received better treatment than plantation field hands.  They were highly valued commodities because of their special expertise and because they could be sold for a higher price.  The types of Negro artisans that could be found on plantations included carpenters, blacksmiths, wheelwrights and seamstresses.

11.  Crum, Mason.  Gulah:  Negro Life in the Carolina Sea Islands. Durham, N.C.:  Duke University Press, 1940.

Chapter 10 describes the plantation mission to the slaves as perceived and promoted by white ministers and planters.  The plantation ministers are portrayed sympathetically, as individuals who cared for the slaves. (This work serves as a useful account of what the white minister and planter sought to teach the slave.)

12. Curry, Leonard P. The Free Black in Urban America, 1800-1850: The Shadow of the Dream. Chicago and London: University of Chicago Press, 1981.

Curry provides a study of free blacks in fifteen cities in the North, Midwest and the South. Chapter 10 focuses on black urban education with primary emphasis on education of the black child and the black youth in public schools, entrepreneurial schools, institutional schools (operated by churches and other organizations) and philanthropic schools; however, mention is also made of evening and Sunday schools for black adults. Of special importance to black adult education is the study of the "associational activities of urban blacks" highlighted in Chapter 12. Curry analyzes the rise of moral reform organizations and literary societies in the urban black centers, especially in the North, and the important role which they played in fostering a sense of community. Curry's study emphasizes the urban black community's "faith in the liberating qualities of education," viewing literacy, intellectual development and moral uplift as the key to both individual and communal advancement.

13. Drake, Thomas. Quakers and Slavery in America. New Haven, Conn.: Yale University Press, 1950.

The Quakers are generally recognized as the religious sect which was most sympathetic to the slaves. They were among the first to free their slaves and to give them educational instruction. This book provides a detailed account of the Quaker-slave relationship.

14. DuBois, W. E. B. The Philadelphia Negro: A Social Study. New York: Benjamin Blom Inc., 1899.

This is a sociological study of the Philadelphia Negro. Of special relevance for the study of black education is Chapter 8, entitled, "Education and Literacy" in which DuBois highlights the efforts of one of the most noted supporters of black education during the Colonial period, Anthony Benezet, in educating both the Negro youth and adults.

15. Eaton, Clement. "Slave-Hiring in the Upper South: A Step Toward Freedom." Mississippi Valley Historical Review, 44:663-678 (March, 1960).

This article addressing the intricacies of slave-hiring points out that the act of hiring-out slaves was an educational tool in and of itself. In addition to acquiring skills on their new job, hired slaves were given more freedom, higher status and the opportunity to become more enlightened as a result of wider exposure. This article addresses the intricacies of slave-hiring.

16. Finkelstein, Barbara. "Reading, Writing, and the Acquisition of Identity in the United States: 1790-1860." In Barbara Finkelstein, ed. Regulated Children/Liberated Children: Education in Psychohistorical

Perspective. New York: Psychohistory Press, 1979, pp. 114-139, see
especially pp. 127-133.

Finkelstein analyzes the meaning of literacy for the black child and
adult, arguing that learning to read constituted for the slave "an
act of self-assertion, a courageous of independence."

17. Franklin, John Hope. The Free Negro in North Carolina, 1790-1860.
Chapel Hill, N.C.: University of North Carolina Press, 1943.

This book includes a section on "Education." The way Negro adults
in North Carolina managed to acquire the rudiments of education
prior to Emancipation is not much different than what occurred in
other Southern states; however, the apprenticeship system may well
have been more significant there than in other places. As in other
states, religious sects were active in Negro education. "Perhaps
the Quakers accomplished more than any other sect in the task of
educating the Negroes." Evening schools and Sabbath schools were
established for the adult population. "In 1850, of the 12,048 free
Negro adults, 5,191 (or 43 per cent) were literate."

18. _____. From Slavery to Freedom. New York: Alfred Knopf,
1947.

The strongest advocates of education for those of African descent
during the Colonial period were the Quakers. The Society for the
Propagation of the Gospel in Foreign Parts was interested in raising
the level of living of blacks as well. Evidence of activities aimed
at educating blacks by these organizations and others can be found
in this book.

19. _____. "James Boon, Free Negro Artisan." Journal of
Negro History, 30:150-180 (April, 1945).

Franklin provides an excellent case study of the appreticeship
training received and of the skills mastered by a skilled artisan
and free Negro in nineteenth-century, antebellum North Carolina.

20. _____. "Slaves Virtually Free in Antebellum North
Carolina." Journal of Negro History, 28:284-310 (July, 1943).

Laws as well as practices of some slave owners in eighteenth-century
North Carolina tended to diminish the severity of slavery and give
rise to a situation where a number of slaves had the opportunity to
move about virtually as free Negroes. The laws stiffened, however,
in the nineteenth century. The lax attitudes had special relevance
for education as groups, such as the Quakers, utilized the
opportunity in teaching adult blacks to read and write. Franklin
is one of the few authors to actually deal with the topic of
literacy training among the slaves.

21. Frazier, E. Franklin. The Free Negro Family. Nashville, Tenn.:
Fisk University Press, 1932.

This is a study of the free Negro family prior to the Civil War.
Education was vital to the cultural and economic progress of the

free Negro family as well as the Negro race. Throughout the book
the author provides evidence of numerous efforts by individuals and
organizations to educate the free Negro adult.

22. Freeman, M. H. "The Educational Wants of the Free Colored People,
1859." Integrated Education, 10:30-34 (January-February, 1972).

This article purports to be a reflection of educational wants of
blacks in 1859. The author provides a prescriptive definition of
education as well.

". . . It is certainly not, as many seem to suppose, merely a large
collection of facts laid up in the storehouse of memory, whence may
be brought forth at any time and in any quantity things new and old.
Nor is it a mere knowledge of languages, mathematics, histories and
philosophies. The various sciences, each and all, may be used as a
means of education, but they are not the education itself.
Education is the harmonious development of the physical, mental and
moral powers of man. . . ."

23. Genovese, Eugene D. Roll Jordan Roll: The World the Slaves Made.
New York: Pantheon Books-Random House, 1972.

Roll Jordan Roll is a monumental work, both in breadth of coverage
and depth of source materials, written by a leading authority on
slavery in America and serves as a standard, if not the standard
work, on the life and culture of the slave. The work seeks to
understand the world which the black slaves made rather than the one
which the slaveowners made. Genovese's work, though written from
the perspective of the slave, is free of stereotypes where all
blacks are portrayed as self-conscious, heroic preservers of their
African culture and where all whites are portrayed as sadistic
taskmasters.

As a study of the world which the slaves made, much of the book is
useful for a study of the education of the adult slave. Genovese
analyzes the process by which the Afro-Americans were able to
develop "their own values as a force for community cohesion and
survival" the success of which "widened the cultural gap" between
themselves and the white Americans. Of special relevance are the
sections on "reading, writing and prospects" describing the desire
for and efforts of slaves to "steal" some literacy; the section on
religion, especially the part dealing with the gospel in the slave
quarters, analyzing the slaves' needs for and ability to reshape
Christianity "to fit their own psychic needs"; and the section on
the "men of skill" analyzing the black craftsmen's ability to serve
as manly examples to black youths and to blend Afro-American with
American elements in their works of art.

24. Golden, Claudia Dale. Urban Slavery in the American South, 1820-
1860: A Quantitative History. Chicago and London: University of
Chicago Press, 1976.

Golden provides an excellent account of the occupations held by
urban slaves, especially in the skilled job sector. Emphasis is

placed on the high level of skills held rather than on the training
received by the urban slaves.

25.  Gross, Bella.  "The First National Convention."  Journal of Negro
History, 31:435-443 (October, 1946).

Gross describes the organization, leadership and policy of the
Convention and its role in educating both the black and white
communities on the race issue prior to the Civil War.

26.  Hull, Gloria T.  But Some of Us Are Brave.  Old Westbury, N.Y.:
The Feminist Press, 1982.

In Chapter 8, "Studying Slavery:  Some Literary and Pedagogical
Considerations on the Black Female Slave," Hull explores the female
slave's education, attitude towards work  and status in the slave
family.  This is one of a very few studies available dealing with
the education of the female slave.

27.  Jackson, Luther P.  Free Negro Labor and Property Holding in
Virginia, 1830-1860.  New York:  Appleton-Century, Co., 1942.

Of special importance is Jackson's study of the free Negro barber
who was among the most highly educated of the members of his race
in Richmond.  Many barbers were literate and "constituted a free
Negro aristocracy."  In a broad sense, Negro barber shops in
Richmond were educational institutions.

28.  _____.  "Religious Development of the Negro in Virginia
From 1760 to 1860."  Journal of Negro History, 16:168-239 (April, 1931).

One of the early contributors to the Journal of Negro History and an
historian whose work was marked by solid research and sound judgment,
Luther P. Jackson merits inclusion in any standard bibliography
dealing with the religious development and instruction of the black
slave.  A student of William Warren Sweet, Jackson's association of
revivalism and the spread of the Baptist churches with the democratic
spirit is dated but his discussion of what the white churches sought
to teach the black slave is excellent.  Jackson traces the beginning
of religious education of Negroes to the Revolutionary era and the
Great Awakening rather than to the efforts of the Society for the
Promotion of Christian Knowledge and the Society for the Propagation
of the Gospel in Foreign Parts.  It was not until the period of
1790-1830 that the organized Negro churches appeared, many of which
were lead by black preachers especially in urban centers.  Jackson
analyzes the impact of the anti-literacy legislation for blacks
after 1832, especially its importance to the use of the oral
catechism method in religious instruction.  Of special note here was
Rev. Robert Ryland's catechism, comprising fifty-two lessons, taught
at regular Sunday services and in the Sunday School, emphasizing
values such as chastity and punctuality.

29.  _____.  "Religious Instruction of Negroes, 1830-1860, With
Special Reference to South Carolina."  Journal of Negro History, 15:72-
114 (January, 1930).

Jackson's sound and balanced account is still a useful starting point in the study of the religious instruction of the slave. Written primarily from the perspective of the white churches it tells us more of what was intended than what was actually appropriated by the slave. Jackson describes the religious instruction activities undertaken by Baptists, Methodists, Presbyterians and Episcopalians including the rise of the plantation mission led by Charles C. Jones. In addition to describing the efforts of white clergymen, Jackson also highlights the efforts of black assistants working with white clergymen in religious instruction. He concludes that the mission to the slave, emphasized by Southern white churches after 1845, did humanize slavery but it did not carry with it any seeds of emancipation.

30. Jernegan, Marcus W. Laboring and Dependent Classes in Colonial America 1607-1783. Chicago: University of Chicago Press, 1931.

During the Colonial period, slaves were provided limited opportunities for educational enlightenment throughout the colonies. The author provides a detailed account of these activities in Chapter 2, "Religious Instruction and Conversion of Negro Slaves."

31. Johnson, Whittington B. "Negro Laboring Classes in Early America, 1750-1820." Ph.D. dissertation, University of Georgia, 1970.

This dissertation examines the subject of "Negro labor in early America." The term "labor" is used in its broadest sense to include all black workers except farmers and farm hands, and includes various skilled occupations.

During the period of 1750-1820, a large percentage of this country's skilled artisans were Negroes. Blacks were trained as barbers, a trade which they dominated, as well as cooks, butchers, canal diggers, chimney sweepers, carpenters, masons, wheelwrights, seamstresses, cobblers, blacksmiths and architects.

32. Jordan, Winthrop D. White Over Black. Chapel Hill, N.C.: University of North Carolina Press, 1968.

Jordan's work is a classic study of racial attitudes, underlying slavery, in America. Of relevance for the study of adult education is his discussion of the Quakers, who, he argues, were the primary catalyst in black education prior to the Civil War.

33. Katz, William L. Eyewitness: The Negro in American History. New York: Pitman Publishing Co., 1967.

Katz emphasizes the contributions of Anthony Benezet to black education, including the education of the old and the young, in Philadelphia.

34. Klingberg, Frank J. An Appraisal of the Negro in Colonial South Carolina. Washington, D.C.: The Associated Publishers, 1941.

Alexander Garden was one of the first advocates of Negro education. He established a school for Negroes in South Carolina which also opened its doors to adults. Garden's contributions are discussed in Chapter 5 which is entitled "The Charleston Negro School."

35.  Lincoln, C. Eric.  The Negro Pilgrimage in America.  New York: Bantam, 1967.

This publication underscores the significance of informal education obtained by slaves through self-employed survival strategies. Despite efforts to keep them illiterate, many slaves were able to defy the odds and obtain the rudiments of education.

36.  Litwack, Leon F.  North of Slavery:  The Negro in the Free States, 1790-1860.  Chicago:  University of Chicago Press, 1961.

The author discusses the experience of the free Negro in America prior to the Civil War.  Provided also is evidence of the many efforts to educate the adult Negro slave by numerous benevolent organizations.

37.  Loring, Edward N.  "Claude C. Jones:  Missionary to Plantation Slaves, 1831-1847."  Ph.D. dissertation, Vanderbilt University, 1976.

Loring analyzes the work of one of the South's foremost missionaries to the slaves.  Of special relevance for the study of the education of the black adult is Chapter 3 where Loring describes both the content and the method of Jones' religious education, including descriptions of the oral method (catechism), the Sunday Schools and the Sermons.  Loring notes the conservative roots of the mission to the slave, especially Jones' emphasis on obedience, thrift, chastity, hard work and temperance, and explores the mission's relationship to the Southern political and social order.

38.  Mathews, Donald G.  Religion in the Old South.  Chicago and London: University  of Chicago Press, 1977.

Mathews' intellectual and religious history includes an excellent analysis  of the evangelicals' mission to the slave, a mission designed to convert both slave and slaveowners to evangelical Christianity and thereby halting the development of two separate cultures in the South.  To accomplish these goals the mission stressed religious instruction and church discipline.  The missionaries sought to convince the slaves that those slaveholders, who became converted, would have their best interests at heart.  In the end the missionaries failed to create their idyllic communities and became, instead, guardians of the status quo.

39.  McGee, Leo.  "Early Black Education," Liberator, 11:4-5 (March, 1971).

"Education for the black American began with adult education." Adult slaves had to learn to survive in their new environment.  The slaves themselves were responsible for much of their education; however, most of the educational opportunities provided those of African descent were by those of lighter skin color.  This article sketches the process of education for black adults in America during the Colonial period.

40. _____. "Early Efforts Toward Educating the Black Adult."
Adult Leadership, 19:341 (April, 1971).

> The article defines adult education as all those educational
> activities designed for adults. Education of black adults in
> America had its beginning in 1619 when twenty black Africans were
> delivered to Jamestown, Virginia. The initial educational methods
> perhaps consisted of observation, trial and error, exchange of
> experiences, along with direction from white colonial leaders
> concerning the labor and service of their newly acquired servants.

> The period 1619-1850 was crucial with respect to black adult
> education. During those years proponents and opponents of black
> education experienced different degrees of success. This article
> cites many examples of successful educational programs for black
> adults in the major cities as well as in more rural areas.

> There was always a number of whites who were against educating
> blacks. This opposition was predicated on the belief that educating
> blacks was not congruent with their position as slaves. This
> skepticism reached its highest point in 1831. That was the year of
> the Nat Turner revolt in Southampton County, Virginia, which
> resulted in the death of over sixty whites.

41. Meier, August, and Elliott Rudwick. From Plantation to Ghetto.
New York: Hill & Wang, 1966.

> The authors consider the generation prior to the Civil War the most
> productive regarding the education of black adults. The book
> identifies a number of the societies that were most effective in
> promoting black education--Society for Propagation of the Gospel,
> New York Manumission Society, Society of Free People of Color for
> Promoting the Instruction and School Education of People of African
> Descent, The New York Society of Free People of Color, Brown
> Fellowship Society and the Minor Society.

> Other organizations that were instrumental in promoting black
> education were the Negro Church (AME Church in particular),
> fraternal organizations, abolitionist societies and the Negro
> Convention Society.

42. Miller, Kelly. Race Adjustment. New York: The Neale Publishing
Company, 1910.

> In the chapter, "The Early Struggle for Education," the author
> explores the uncertainties surrounding the educational struggle of
> the oppressed.

43. Moon, Sandra L. "A Successful 19th Century Literary Society."
Negro History Bulletin, 41:850 (July-August, 1978).

> The article provides a brief description of the efforts of the
> Philadelphia Library Company of Colored Persons, organized in 1833,
> in elevating the black community, intellectually and culturally.

44. Mooney, Chase C. <u>Slavery in Tennessee</u>. Bloomington, Ind.: Indiana University Press, 1957.

The author credits the Methodist Church as being the most active denomination in religious work among the slaves in Tennessee. The efforts of churches in providing religious instruction is high-lighted, as the following quotation exemplifies:

"While there were a number of separate churches for the Negroes, the more usual practice was to give religious instruction to the slave on the premises of the owner, or in the churches of the whites, where they occupied the back rows or the balcony . . . it is the practice of a number of ministers to preach to the Negroes separately on the Sabbath or during the week. There are also Sabbath schools in some of the churches for children and adults, and in all the houses of worship, with a few exceptions, a greater or less number of colored members and Negroes form a portion of every Sabbath congregation. . . ."

45. Morgan, T. J. <u>The Negro American</u>. Philadelphia: American Baptist Publication Society, 1898.

This book discusses the educational shortcomings of Negroes during slavery, but acknowledges that some were able to acquire rudimentary skill through the efforts of benevolent whites.

46. Ottley, Roi. <u>Black Odyssey</u>. New York: Scribner's Sons, 1948.

The Quakers were omnipresent in the lives of Negroes throughout the Colonial period. They spoke out against slavery and were proponents of Negro education. A section of this book deals with the efforts of the Quakers in Christianizing the Negro.

47. Pease, William H., and Jane H. Pease. <u>Black Utopia: Negro Communal Experiments in America</u>. Madison, Wis.: The State Historical Society, 1963.

The authors argue that Negro communal experiments in the nineteenth century, unlike their non-Negro counterparts, were not built on the European communal traditions of socialism and communism but were firmly based upon the American middle-class philosophy of self-reliance, individualism, independence and capitalism.

48. _____. "Organized Negro Communities: A North American Experiment." <u>Journal of Negro History</u>, 47:10-34 (January, 1962).

The authors analyze the reasons for and problems of organized Negro communities in Canada and the United States from the American Revolution to the end of the Civil War. They point out that one reason for the establishment of the communities was the blacks' desire for education, including the desire to establish schools and manual labor schools, to provide opportunities for the training of religious leaders and to promote the moral uplift of all blacks.

49. Perlman, Daniel. "Organizations of the Free Negro in New York City, 1800-1860." <u>Journal of Negro History</u>, 56:181-197 (July, 1971).

Perlman analyzes the organized efforts of blacks "free of white help, intervention, or explortation," to improve their own lot in New York City.  Included in the study are four benevolent self-help societies: The New York African Society for Mutual Relief, the Wilberforce Philanthropic Society of New York, the African-Tompkins Association and the African Clarkson Association.

50.  Pih, Richard W.  "Negro Self-Improvement Efforts in Ante-Bellum Cincinnati, 1836-1850."  Ohio History, 78:179-187 (Summer, 1969).

This article addresses an area of Negro well-being that has received little attention by historians, namely Negro self-improvement efforts prior to 1860.  While an unlimited number of white organizations assisted in Negro education throughout history, self-help programs were equally as significant.

51.  Porter, Dorothy.  "The Organized Educational Activities of Negro Literary Societies, 1828-1846."  Reprinted in August Meier and Elliott Rudwick, eds. The Making of Black America:  Essays in Negro Life and History, Vol. I.  The Origins of Black America.  Studies in American Negro Life. New York:  Antheneum, 1969.  Pp. 276-288.

Porter provides an excellent descriptive study of black literary societies in New York and Philadelphia.  She surveys their efforts in disseminating knowledge, sponsoring lectures, and notes their emphasis on adult literacy.  Porter concludes that the societies "were supporters of the educative life among Negroes in a day when there were few formal instruments of education in existence for their use."  It is definitely one of the better articles on black adult education published prior to World War II.

52.  Rammelkamp, Julian.  "The Providence Negro Community, 1820-1842." Rhode Island History, 7:20-33 (January, 1948).

Rammelkamp provides an excellent analysis of the origin and establishment of a pre-Civil War community including a description of the black community's efforts to educate its people.  He discusses the educational efforts of churches, schools and religious and secular societies in educating both the adults and the young.

53.  Rector, Theodore A.  "Black Nuns as Educators."  Journal of Negro Education, 51:238-253 (Summer, 1982).

Rector makes brief mention of black nuns providing instruction in "faith and morals" for black adults in New Orleans prior to the Civil War and offering night classes to freedmen during Reconstruction.

54.  Redding, Saunders.  They Came in Chains.  Philadelphia:  J. B. Lippincott Co., 1950.

The work of Anthony Benezet in Philadelphia regarding Negro adult education is mentioned.  The author also points out that many blacks were educated at the African Free School in New York between 1787 and 1815.

55. Robbins, Gerald. "William F. Allen: Classical Scholar Among the Slaves." History of Education Quarterly, 5:211-223 (December, 1963).

This is a story of William F. Allen during his tenure as a teacher among the slaves on the South Carolina sea islands. Allen was a classical Harvard scholar. He and his family spent several years on the islands, and there he and his wife provided instruction for the old and young.

56. Russell, John H. The Free Negro in Virginia, 1619-1865. Baltimore: Johns Hopkins University Press, 1913.

This book gives an excellent account of the educational opportunities accorded the free Negro in Virginia from 1619-1865. Much of the education provided those of African descent was religious training. The strongest religious advocates of Negro education were the Quakers, Methodists, Moravians, Harmonites, Shakers and Baptists. In addition to religious training many Negroes received apprentice- ship training in special skills, enabling some to become successful artisans.

57. Stampp, Kenneth M. The Peculiar Institution: Slavery in the Antebellum South. New York: Alfred A. Knopf, 1956.

Stampp explores the impact of slavery on the slave community, family and religion. He focuses primarily on what white society sought to teach the slave and concludes that slavery stripped away most of the slave's African heritage and gave in return little more than vocational training.

58. Starobin, Robert. "Disciplining Industrial Slaves in the Old South." Journal of Negro History, 53:111-128 (April, 1968).

Starobin analyzes the methods used to discipline and control industrial slaves including the use of Christian indoctrination.

59. Stavisky, Leonard P. "The Negro Artisan in the South Atlantic States, 1800-1860: A Study of Status and Economic Opportunity with Special Reference to Charleston." Ph.D. dissertation, Columbia University, 1958.

Chapter 2, "Artisans at Work," contains a useful section on the appreticeship system for children, youth and young adults. Stavisky points out that most skills taught in the apprenticeship system were elementary in nature, although some slaves learned to produce work of high quality and acquired expert knowledge.

60. _____. "The Origins of Negro Craftsmanship in Colonial America." Journal of Negro History, 32:417-429 (October, 1947).

Stavisky provides an excellent account of the reasons for and methods of training male and female in various crafts during the Colonial era. He concludes that by the time of the American Revolution slaves were represented in every trade.

61.  Sternett, Michael.  Black Religion and American Evangelism:  White Protestants, Plantation Missions, and the Flowering of Negro Christianity, 1787-1865.  ATLA Monograph Series No. 7.  Metuchen, N.J.:  Scarecrow Press, 1975.  Chapters 2, 6.

> Most useful for the study of adult education is Chapter 2 which focuses on the gospel for slaves as viewed by the white missionary. Sternett discusses the methods of instruction, the oral catechism and the content of instruction which emphasized cleanliness, the sanctity of the family, duty, docility, honesty and fidelity. Chapter 6 focuses on the black churches' emphasis on similar values of cleanliness, thrift, industry, temperance, marital fidelity and charity towards the less fortunate as well as the African Methodist Episcopal Church's efforts in the education of ministers.

62.  Taylor, Orville W.  Negro Slavery in Arkansas.  Durham, N.C.:  Duke University Press, 1958.

> In Chapter 10, "Readin, 'Ritin,' and Religion," the author highlights the educational activities of various groups, especially of the Catholic, Methodist and Baptist churches.

63.  Vibert, Faith.  "The Society for the Propagation of the Gospel in Foreign Parts:  Its Work for Negroes in North America before 1783." Journal of Negro History,  18:171-212 (April, 1933).

> Vibert highlights the efforts of the Society, especially of the catechist in New York City, in instructing children and adults in the three decades preceeding the American Revolution.

64.  Wade, Richard C.  Slavery in the Cities:  The South, 1820-1860. New York:  Oxford University Press, 1964.

> One of the first major studies on urban slavery, Wade's work includes two brief sections that have relevance for the study of adult education.  The first section explores the opportunities for literacy training and the role of the urban church as nurseries of self government for blacks.  The second section explores the declining opportunity for apprenticeship training and job placement in skilled and semi-skilled trades after 1830.

65.  Webber, Thomas L.  Deep Like the Rivers:  Education in the Slave Quarter Community, 1831-1865.  New York:  W. W. Norton, 1978.

> Webber's work, a social, intellectual and educational history of the Afro-American in the slave community, relies heavily on records left by slaves themselves to address three major questions:  What did white society seek to teach the slave?  What did the slave learn? From whom did the slaves receive that which they actually learned?

> In his attempt to analyze that which the slaves internalized and which gave meaning to their existence he focuses on the importance of the family, the peer group, the slave congregation, slave songs and stories and the slave community in the creation of a slave culture which gave meaning to life and fashioned a world-view different from that of white society.

Webber's work is one of the best available studies on the education or acculturization of the slave.

66.  Wesley, Charles H.  International Library of Negro Life and History--In Freedom's Footsteps.  New York:  Publishers Co. Inc., 1968.

In one section of this pictorial work, the author dwells on the "Education of the Free Negro," in which he cites some of the most effective individuals and organizations.

67.  Whatley III, George C.  "The Alabaman Presbyterian and His Slave, 1830-1864."  The Alabama Review, 13:40-51 (January, 1960).

Whatley provides a fairly complete descriptive study of the Presbyterian Church's role in religious education of the slave, including its use of oral instruction.  The Presbyterian Church's impact was limited, however, never reaching more than two percent of Alabama's slave population.

68.  White, Arthur O.  "The Black Leadership Class and Education in Antebellum Boston."  Journal of Negro Education, 42:504-515 (Fall, 1973).

This article contains a brief account of Negro adult education in Antebellum Boston.

69.  Woodson, Carter G.  The Education of the Negro Prior to 1861.  New York:  Arno Press, 1968.

In this study, Woodson concentrates on the broad scope of black education, touching sparingly on adult education.  Of the multitude of efforts of benevolent organizations to educate blacks during the Colonial period, most were predicated on religious conviction.  The Bible became a vital instructional tool in teaching blacks to read and to become proficient in religious interpretation and under-standing.

When slaves first entered the new world they had to become educated immediately for sheer survival and to become familiar with their labor assignments.  Plantation owners later discovered that skilled slaves were of great value to the plantation itself and a profitable investment for the slave system.  Trained slaves could be sold for higher prices as well as significantly improve the operation of the plantation.  This type of apprenticeship training for selected slaves was instituted on nearly all plantations.  Those plantations that did not have their own training programs were able to benefit from others through the availability of trained slaves at auctions and the possibility of having slaves sent out for training and work assignments.

70.  _____.  The Negro in Our History.  Washington, D.C.:  The Associated Publishers Inc., 1922.

Elias Neau of New York and Anthony Benezet of Philadelphia are considered the most prominent Negro adult educators during the Colonial period.  They were operating schools for Negro adults in

their respective cities as early as 1706 and 1750.  The author
describes their contributions and explores other clandestine
strategies used to educate the Afro-Americans.

71.   _____.  "The Negroes of Cincinnati Prior to the Civil War."
Journal of Negro History, 1:1-22 (January, 1916).

Carter describes the successful efforts of the Cincinnati black
community to establish itself economically and educationally prior
to the Civil War in the face of increased racism and the passage of
Black Laws.  The educational work for adults consisted of writing
and evening schools.  Black churches and Sunday Schools promoted
literacy, religion and moral development.  In addition some blacks
mastered a trade and became mechanics.

72.  Wright, James M.  The Free Negro in Maryland, 1634-1860.  New York:
Columbia University, 1921.

The free Negro was always the advantaged one when compared to others
of his race.  The author points out that in the State of Maryland
educational instruction was provided for the free children as well
as adults.  Most was provided by religious sects, i.e., Quakers and
Methodists.

# 2
# CIVIL WAR AND
# RECONSTRUCTION, 1860–1880

73. Anderson, James D. "Ex-Slaves and the Rise of Universal Education in the New South, 1860-1880." In Ronald K. Goodenow and Arthur White, eds., Education and the Rise of the New South. Boston: G. K. Hall, 1981. Pp. 1-25.

The author analyzes the reasons underlying the ex-slaves' thirst for literacy and describes the early attempts by ex-slaves to set up freedmen's schools. Emphasis is placed on the black community's early involvement in setting up schools, including Sabbath schools. The freedmen are depicted not as unrealistic, child-like seekers after the trappings of white society but rather as a "responsible and politically self-conscious, social class."

74. Armstrong, Warren B. "Union Chaplains and the Education of the Freedmen." Journal of Negro History, 52:104-115 (April, 1967).

Union chaplains were among the strongest proponents of Negro education during the Civil War years. They fought long and hard for a national policy in Negro education. Many took it upon themselves to instruct those who had come behind Union lines. They became an integral factor in the Negro's struggle for "education, economic stability, and social equality and acceptance." They argued that education was essential if Negroes were to make the transition from slaves to responsible citizens.

Eventually, Congress enacted legislation which created the Freedmen's Bureau. This article speaks to the vital contribution Union chaplains made toward the improvement of the quality of life of former slaves.

75. Bahney, Robert Stanley. "Generals and Negroes: Education of Negroes by the Union Army, 1861-1865." Ph.D. dissertation, University of Michigan, 1965.

The study describes and analyzes the experiments in Negro education undertaken by General Rufus Saxton and the Department of the South,

General Benjamin Butler and the Department of North Carolina and
Virginia, General Ulysses Grant and Chaplain John Eaton and the
Department of Tennessee and Arkansas and General Nathaniel Banks
and the Department of the Gulf.  Lacking any systematic plans or
educational administrations, the experiments were undertaken
primarily to deal with the influx of thousands of slaves into
Union lines and Army camps.

Of special interest are the diverse policies established by the
different armies.  Whereas General Grant and John Eaton solved the
"contraband" problem by separating the blacks from the soldiers
and setting up special contraband camps where the blacks received
clothing, tools and materials, enabling them to work for the
Northern government and private citizens, General Nathan Banks
sought to encourage the blacks to stay at home on the land by
providing them with clothing and schools on the plantations.

Although a good analysis of Union Army policies, the study sheds
relatively little light on the content of the programs themselves
and on the blacks' aspirations for participating in or even their
response to the programs.

76.  Bentley, George R.  "A History of the Freedmen's Bureau."  Ph.D.
dissertation, University of Wisconsin, 1948.

The Freedmen's Bureau was established specifically to deal with
affairs of the recently freed black population.  Education was one
of its major thrusts.  This dissertation is a comprehensive study
of the Bureau.

77.  _____.  A History of the Freedmen's Bureau.  Philadelphia:
University of Pennsylvania Press, 1955.

One of the earlier accounts of the Freedmen's Bureau, Bentley's
History was written prior to the studies of the Bureau's activities
in various states which were published during and after the Civil
Rights Movement of the 1960's.  Bentley provides a critical analysis
of the Bureau's efforts in promoting and supporting black education
as well as of its involvement in Republican politics.  The freedmen's thirst for literacy and the opposition of Southern whites to
freedmen's schools is analyzed.  Bentley discusses the Bureau's
contributions to freedmen's education:  it provided psychological
support to missionary organizations, leadership, buildings for
schools and encouraged benevolent societies to establish normal
schools and colleges for the freedmen and to promote moral
education.  The author, however, is critical of the Bureau's
involvement in politics, arguing that its radical political
activities fanned the flames of Southern white opposition and
negated much of its good work.

78.  Billington, Ray Allen.  The Journal of Charlotte L. Forten.
New York:  Dryden Press, 1953.

This publication includes the journal of one of the early Yankee
"schoolmarms" in the South during the Civil War including a
perspective introduction by Ray Billington.  Mention is made of

selected black adults' eagerness to learn. The journal is important
for the insights it provides of the attitudes held by Northern
missionaries relative to the freedmen.

79. Blassingame, John. "Before the Ghetto: The Making of the Black
Community in Savannah Georgia, 1865–1880." Journal of Social History,
6:463–488 (Summer, 1973).

    Blassingame provides an excellent study of the building and
    education of a black community following the Civil War. In order to
    diffuse knowledge, essential for the establishment of a viable
    community and faced with the unwillingness of the Chatham County
    Board of Education to establish schools for blacks prior to 1872,
    Savannah blacks were forced to take the initiative in establishing
    their own schools. Blassingame analyzes the black community's
    efforts in establishing their own schools, the role played by black
    churches in promoting education, racial pride, self-respect and
    morality, including the need for stable families, and describes the
    blacks' successful attempts in organizing nearly 200 clubs and
    mutual aid societies. He underscores the importance of the
    promotion of literacy for the building of a viable black community.

80. _____. Black New Orleans, 1860–1880. Chicago and London:
University of Chicago Press, 1973.

    Although adult education is not emphasized in Blassingame's
    excellent social history of the New Orleans' black community during
    these two decades, he does make mention of efforts undertaken by
    whites and especially by blacks to educate the black community.
    Mention is made of the relatively high rate of free Negroes in
    skilled occupations prior to the Civil War, and of the Union Army's
    deliberate attempt to teach black soldiers to read during the Civil
    War. Chapter 5 is devoted to the establishment of schools and
    colleges as well as to the rise of Negro newspapers. Of special
    importance for the study of adult education is Blassingame's
    analysis of the importance of the "social life" activities of the
    black community (Chapter 6), including churches, lectures and clubs
    in cultivating literary tastes and sponsoring public debate. An
    important study, it points the historian beyond the school house or
    college to other institutions and clubs when dealing with the
    education of the black adult.

81. _____. "Negro Chaplains in the Civil War." Negro History
Bulletin, 27:23,24 (October, 1963).

    Blassingame provides a brief description of the efforts of Negro
    Chaplains in the Union Army, not only in conducting religious
    services and officiating at funerals but also in providing moral
    instruction and literacy training for black soldiers many of whom
    were illiterate ex-slaves.

82. _____. "The Union Army as an Educational Institution for
Negroes, 1862–1865." Journal of Negro Education, 34:152–159 (Spring,
1965).

Blassingame provides an excellent, concise description of the Union
Army's role in the education of the blacks during the Civil War.  He
highlights and describes the efforts of the army generals and
chaplains in providing literacy training and moral education as well
as military drill for black soldiers both from the South and the
North.  Blassingame concludes that thousands of black soldiers
received their first supervised instruction from and learned to read
in the Union Army.

83.  Bond, Horace Mann.  The Education of the Negro in the American
Social Order.  New York:  Octagon Books, 1966.

Although this book is devoted almost exclusively to the education of
the young, the author did make mention of the strong desire by black
adults for an education following the Civil War.  "At no time or
place in America has been exemplified so pathetic a faith in
education as the lever of racial  progress.  Grown men studied their
alphabets in the fields, holding the 'blue-back speller' with one
hand while they guided the plow with the other."  The Union Army
played a significant role in the education of Negro adults as well.

84.  _____.  Negro Education in Alabama:  A Study in Cotton and
Steel.  Washington, D.C.:  The Associated Publishers, 1939.

Written by one of the most noted black scholars prior to World War
II, this study is devoted primarily to the study of the education
of the Negro youth in Alabama; however, Bond also briefly describes
provisions for education of Negro adults made by the Freedmen's
Bureau and the Mission societies.

85.  Botume, Elizabeth Hyde.  First Days Amongst the Contrabands.  New
York:  Arno Press-The New York Times, 1968 [1893].

This is an account by a Yankee "schoolmarm" on Port Royal Islands
during the Civil War and Reconstruction.  Although Botume describes
many of her impressions of the freedmen, including their poverty and
religion, she also devotes much of her attention to the education of
the Island blacks, both young and old.  Emphasis is placed upon the
black adult's thirst for education, depicted as often being
superficial and unrealistic.  The impression one receives is of
black adults flitting in and out of schools once the crops were
cultivated hoping to quickly catch some learning.  The freedmen are
viewed with compassion but also portrayed as a "childlike" people.
The missionaries' attempts to create ebony Puritans by emphasizing
values such as cleanliness, thrift and frugality are evident.  An
important account, it provides insight into the Northern missionaries'
perceptions of what the ex-slaves were  and what they ought to
become.

86.  Brown, Ira V.  "Lyman Abbott and the Freedmen's Aid, 1865-1869."
Journal of Southern History, 15:22-38 (February, 1949).

The essay describes Lyman Abbott's and the American Freedmen's Union
Commission's efforts in and goals for black education.  Although
it does not focus on adult education per se, the article is important
in that it highlights the non denominational organization's efforts

in relief and education as well as its concept of black education for suffrage and job training for skilled-labor positions.

87.  Castel, Albert.  "Civil War Kansas and the Negro." Journal of Negro History, 51:125-138 (April, 1966).

Castel discusses the experiences of the fugitive Negroes who congregated in the more populated areas of Kansas including Leavenworth, Lawrence, Wyadoth and Fort Scott.  At least one school that catered to adults was established in Lawrence.  "In December, 1861, the night school which had been established for the illiterate ex-slaves had 83 pupils ranging from old men to young children."

88.  Cornish, Dudley T.  The Sable Arm:  Negro Troops in the Union Army, 1861-1865.  New York:  W. W. Norton, 1966.

The history of the Negro soldier in the Union Army is more than merely a military history.  Separate histories could be written of the Negro's recruitment, training, attitude, treatment and employment.  This comprehensive volume attempts to address all of these areas and others.

The purpose of this study is not to prove that the Civil War could not have been won without the support of Negro troops.  Rather, its primary intent is to show the difficulties involved in and the obstacles encountered by the gradual move to arm the Negro; to analyze the process of emergence of the Negro soldier as a member of the Union Army; and, to assess his contribution to the Army and to the outcome of the War.

89.  _____.  "The Union Army as a School for Negroes." Journal of Negro History, 37:368-382 (October, 1952).

Cornish provides an excellent discussion on the Union Army's role in providing formal education for black troops.  Although the Union Army, itself, had no overall educational program for black troops, many officers did recognize and attempt to fulfill the black soldiers' need and desire for literacy.  Cornish surveys the experiments in black education carried on in various sectors and by numerous officers.  He concludes that given the demands of officers' time for military drill, it is surprising how much education of black troops did actually take place.

90.  Cruden, Robert.  The Negro in Reconstruction.  Englewood Cliffs, N.J.:  Prentice-Hall, 1969.

By the author's own admission, this book is not a comprehensive history of the Reconstruction Period.  It attempts to demonstrate the Negroes' struggle to "find meaning in freedom."  An excellent account of the Union Army's effort in Negro education is presented:

". . . The Black regiments were almost entirely illiterate; white officers found it an essential part of their duty to teach black noncommissioned officers how to write and figure.  'School tents' were set up in all Negro outfits, through which thousands of blacks received their introduction to education."

91.  Donald, Henderson H.   The Negro Freedman.   New York:   Henry Schuman,
Inc., 1952.

> During the Civil War, thousands of slaves sought shelter themselves
> behind Union lines.   Their strong desire for an education caught the
> attention of Army officials who in turn made this known to philan-
> thropic and religious organizations throughout the Northeast.   In
> later years the Federal Government gave some attention to this
> matter through the Freedmen's Bureau.   This book cites examples of
> efforts made to educate the Negro adult, i.e.:
>
> "At Hampton, Norfolk, and Portsmouth, Virginia, day and Sabbath
> schools for the Negroes were conducted in the colored churches;
> evening schools for adults were established, and men and women
> flocked to them after performing their arduous duties of the day."

92.  Drake, Richard B.   "The American Missionary and the Southern Negro,
1861-1888."   Ph.D. dissertation, Emory University, 1957.

> The American Missionary Association, along with other of its peer
> associations, provided the impetus for the creation of many programs
> for the education of the black adult population.   This dissertation
> provides an excellent account of such activities.

93.  DuBois, W. E. B.   Black Reconstruction in America.   New York:
Russell and Russell, 1962.

> Among the strongest desires of the black masses following the Civil
> War was the desire for an education.   The three factions primarily
> responsible for instituting educational programs for blacks of all
> ages were blacks themselves, the Federal Government (through the
> Freedmen's Bureau) and Northern benevolents.   Many day and evening
> schools, including schools for adults, were established.   This book
> identifies and describes many of these programs.

94.  Elliott, Claude.   "The Freedmen's Bureau in Texas."   The South-
western Historical Quarterly, 56:1-24 (July, 1952).

> Elliott argues that the Freedmen's Bureau achieved few successes in
> its five-year history in Texas aside from education.   Despite white
> opposition, black day, evening and Sunday schools were established,
> enrolling not only children but also adults, and providing literacy
> and religious training.   Black schools, however, reached only a small
> segment of the black population throughout the five-year period.

95.  Fen, Sing-nan.   "Notes on the Education of Negroes in North
Carolina During the Civil War."   Journal of Negro Education, 36:24-31
(Winter, 1967).

> In this article the author describes the efforts during the Civil
> War to educate the Negro adult in North Carolina.

96.  Franklin, John Hope.   Reconstruction After the Civil War.   Chicago:
University of Chicago Press, 1961.

This book mentions several sources of educational advancement for
the Negro adult including the Freedmen's Bureau, Negro conventions
and Negro churches.

97.   Gaines, Wesley J.   The Negro and the White Man.   Philadelphia:
A.M.E. Publishing House, 1897.

The author contends that the education provided the Negro during and
prior to the Civil War was temporary.  Following the War efforts to
educate the freedmen became more formal.  The strongest efforts in
this regard were made by the Freedmen's Bureau, American Missionary
Association, Western Freedmen's Aid Commission, American Baptist
Home Mission Society, United Presbyterians, Reformed Presbyterians,
the United Brethren in Christ, the Northwestern Freedmen's Aid
Commission and the National Freedmen's Association.  Educational
opportunities were also provided for Negro adults.

98.   Higginson, Thomas Wentworth.   Army Life in a Black Regiment.   East
Lansing, Mich.:  Michigan State University Press, 1960.

Higginson portrays the black soldiers as "docile, gay, and lovable"
children with an inexhaustible thirst for learning.

99.   Howard, Victor B.   "The Struggle for Equal Education in Kentucky,
1866-1884."  Journal of Negro Education, 46:305-328 (Fall, 1977).

Of particular interest in this article is the description of a
school for Negro  ex-soldiers, established by John G. Fee, a pioneer
in the struggle for education of freedmen, at Camp Nelson.

100.   James, Felix.   "The Establishment of Freedmen's Village in
Arlington, Virginia."  Negro History Bulletin, 33:90-93 (April, 1970).

James describes the establishment of a village for contrabands
outside Washington, D.C., including its educational provisions for
adults.

101.   Johnson, Guion Griffis.   "Southern Paternalism toward Negroes
after Emancipation."  Journal of Southern History, 23:483-509 (November,
1957).

Johnson is one of the few scholars who focuses on the attitudes of
Southern  whites rather than on the goals and aspirations of
ex-slaves or Northern missionaries.  He categorizes the Southern
white's attitudes to black education in five models ranging from
benevolence to overt opposition.

102.   Jones, Allen W.   "The Black Press in the 'New South':  Jesse C.
Duke's Struggle for Justice and Equality."  Journal of Negro History,
64:215-228 (Summer, 1969).

Following the Civil War, black journalism brought a new dimension to
the lives of former slaves.  They could now get a clear view of the
major issues of the day from a black perspective.  One of the most
aggressive Negro journalists in the South was Jessee Chisholm Duke,

founder of the Montgomery Herald. This article is devoted to this
writer's struggle for justice and equality for his comrades.

103.  Jones, Jacqueline. Soldiers of Light and Love: Northern Teachers
and Georgia Blacks, 1865-1873. Chapel Hill, N.C.: University of North
Carolina Press, 1980.

White teachers from the North flocked to Georgia, as they did to
other Southern states following the Civil War, to assist the
millions of freed blacks in their transition from slaves to freedmen.
Although their major efforts were in educational instruction, they
helped blacks in other ways as well to improve their quality of
life.  Numerous educational programs were sponsored by various
freedmen's aid societies with teachers providing the instructional
and managerial  services.  Programs were available for the young and
old.

Although Jones' focus is first and foremost on the Northern white
females who came South to teach Georgia's blacks, she provides
useful material for the study of black adult education as well.  One
finds information on the efforts by blacks to establish their own
educational institutions, including their collaboration with the
Federal Government and the freedmen's aid societies.

104.  Jones, Thomas J.  "Negro Education." U.S. Bureau of Education
Bulletin No. 38.  Washington, D.C.:  Government Printing Office, 1916.
Pp. 289, 296, 297.

This report includes a list of Northern and Negro organizations that
contributed to the educational cause of the Negro during the 1860's
and 1870's.  Many of these resources were used to establish
educational programs for adults.  The report also addresses the
subject of "Freedmen Aid Societies and Government Cooperation."

105.  Kilchin, Peter.  First Freedom.  Westport, Conn.:  Greenwood Press,
1972.

This book deals specifically with blacks in Alabama from Emancipation
through Reconstruction.  Chapter 4, "The Coming of Black Education,"
addresses the issue of education in the state.  The author reports
that there were limited educational opportunities available to Negro
adults in Alabama.  For example, "the establishment of special night
schools for adults enabled persistent freedmen to attend school
without cutting down on their daily labors."

106.  Littlefield, Daniel F., and Patricia W. McGraw.  "The Arkansas
Freedman, 1869-1870:  Birth of the Black Press in Arkansas." Phylon,
40:75-85 (Spring, 1979).

June, 1869, was the month The Arkansas Freedman was born.  Though
short-lived, it was the first newspaper for blacks in Arkansas and
became a major vehicle for educating the black adult public.

107.  Litwack, Leon F.  Been in the Storm So Long:  The Aftermath of
Slavery.  New York:  Alfred A. Knopf, 1980.

Chapter 9, "The Gospel and the Primer," includes a sensitive and lucid discussion of the uses of the gospel and literacy as perceived by white missionaries and by ex-slaves. Of special relevance is Litwack's analysis of the values promoted by white missionaries both in the church and in the schoolhouse as well as the important role played by black ministers in politicizing and educating the freedmen. Also important is Litwack's analysis of the reasons for the ex-slaves' thirst for literacy and the link between literacy and freedom.

108. Lovett, Bobby L. "The Negro in Tennessee, 1861-1866: A Socio-Military History of the Civil War Era." Ph.D. dissertation, University of Arkansas, 1978.

In addition to the education Negro soldiers and civilians received simply from being a participant in the Civil War, many were assigned to sophisticated training programs. Some soldiers and civilians were employed in the departments of quartermaster, engineering, subsistence and medicine, while others were employed as waterboys, cooks, laundresses, nurses, teamsters, servants, cotton pickers, riverboat hands and general laborers.

This dissertation deals specifically with the Tennessee Negroes' participation in the Civil War from 1861 to 1866. It also analyzes and describes the Union Army's participation in the education of the Negro.

109. _____. "The Negro's Civil War in Tennessee, 1861-1865," Journal of Negro History, 61:36-50 (January, 1976).

This article points out that in addition to enlisting Negroes as soldiers, the Union Army hired thousands as Army laborers. The Army retrained their new employees for positions in such departments as Quartermaster, Subsistence and Engineering.

110. McGee, Leo. "Adult Education for the Black Man in America, 1860-1880: An Historical Study of the Types." Ph.D. dissertation, Ohio State University, 1972.

The period 1860 through 1880 represents a traumatic period in the history of the black man both in his role as a slave and in his educational preparation for the role as a free man. During the Civil War and Reconstruction period many benevolent individuals and organizations attempted to provide education for his enlightenment while a slave and as a free man. During this period education was viewed by blacks as the most significant element for their uplift. When schools were provided, there was a general rush by blacks to quench their thirst for knowledge. Such an ardent desire by blacks for knowledge has never been witnessed elsewhere in American History.

This study describes the economic, psychological, social and political conditions in America that generated education for the black adult during the period 1860 through 1880. It also identifies and describes the types of adult education which were established during this period and identifies organizations and certain of the personalities who recognized the need for such activity and made efforts to encourage the education of the black adult.

111. _____. "Twenty Years of Education for the Black Adult: Implications for Teachers and Administrators." Adult Leadership, 21: 291-294 (March, 1973).

The period 1860 through 1880 represents a traumatic period in history for the black man regarding his role as a slave and his educational preparation for his role as a free man. During the Civil War and the reconstruction period many individuals and organizations attempted to provide education for his enlightenment. The early advocates of education for black people were of four classes: first, masters who desired to increase the economic efficiency of their labor supply; second, sympathetic persons who wished to help the oppressed; third, zealous missionaries who believed that the message of divine love comes equally to all; and fourth, ambitious blacks who aspired to a better life.

The article illuminates this twenty-year period as it relates to the types of educational opportunities available to black adults. It describes many of the benevolent gestures made by numerous organizations, including religious groups, Union Army, Freedman's Bureau, Freedmen's Societies and the Black Press.

The article has implications for all individuals engaged in any form of adult education, whether they be teacher, administrator, program planner, counselor or student. This work should provide the adult educator in particular with a useful supplementary tool which will help him become more effective in organizing the past as it relates to the black adult, curriculum development, methods and techniques of instruction and the conceptualization and administration of adult education programs.

112. McPherson, James M. "The New Puritanism: Values and Goals of Freedmen's Education in America." In Lawrence Stone, ed. The University in Society, II. Princeton: Princeton University Press, 1974. Pp. 611-639.

Although McPherson's focus is primarily on the secondary schools and colleges established by missionary education societies, his summary of the values promoted in Freedmen's schools is applicable for the study of adult education as well. The missionaries viewed their mission as one-directional; the black should learn from the white missionary but the missionary need not learn anything from the freedman. However, the missionaries' contributions, especially their motive of education for eventual equality, are recognized.

113. Meyers, John B. "The Education of Alabama Freedmen During Presidential Reconstruction, 1865-1867." Journal of Negro Education, 40:163-171 (Spring, 1971).

This article provides an account of the benevolent organizations that flooded Alabama as they did other Southern states to assist Negroes in their struggle for an education. The following quotation graphically illustrates the black adults' quest for knowledge:

". . . Many of the old blacks wanted to learn to read the Bible
before they died . . . an old white-haired man was among the
children in a freedmen's school in Mobile. . . . Tottering old men
and women sat side by side with their children and grandchildren
endeavoring to learn their letters.  Adult freedmen used every spare
moment to learn.  It was not uncommon to see them studying the
alphabet during rest periods and after work. . . 'There is some-
thing very touching about seeing the extreme eagerness of the old
freedmen to learn when it can be of little use to them now.'"

114.  Morris, Robert C.  Reading, 'Riting, and Reconstruction:  The
Education of Freedmen in the South, 1861-1870.  Chicago and London:
University of Chicago Press, 1981.

Morris' work provides a concise analysis of the organizations and
individuals involved with and the goals and content of the freedmen's education during Reconstruction.  Morris surveys the religious
and philanthropic organizations, and discusses the work and
aspirations of the Yankee, black and Southern white teachers who
were involved in freedmen's education.  He points to the ideology of
self-help and gradualism prevalent in freedmen's education including
the adult educational activities promoted by the Freedmen's Bureau.
Of special interest is his analysis of the content of books and
curriculum in children's and adult programs.

Morris concludes that although many teachers supported suffrage,
their idealism and lofty goals were tempered by their perceived need
for sectional accommodation.  In the end, freedmen's schools
stressed gradualism and self-improvement assuming that prejudice
would diminish as blacks' self-improvement became evident.

115.  Newsome, A. R.  Studies in History and Political Science.  Chapel
Hill, N.C.:  University of North Carolina Press, 1947.

This is volume number twenty-eight of the Sprunt series published by
the University of North Carolina Sesquicentennial Publications and
deals with "The Negro in Mississippi, 1865-1890."  In Chapter 2,
entitled "From Bondage to Freedom:  The Federal Army and the Negro,"
the author briefly describes the efforts of Army chaplains and
benevolent organizations to educate the Negro soldier and others of
his race who had flocked behind Union lines.

116.  Nolen, Claude H.  The Negro's Image in the South.  Lexington, Ky.:
University of Kentucky Press, 1967.

Chapter 8 is entitled "Control of Education During Reconstruction."
It focuses on education of the Negro following the Civil War:

"After Emancipation Negroes of all ages and degrees of intelligence
displayed unrestrained eagerness for education and made remarkable
efforts to learn, flocking to schools wherever established . . .
Northern teachers pressed into the South behind advancing Union
armies and founded schools in towns and on plantations. . . . They
were supported by seventy-nine freedmen's aid societies and the
Freedman's Bureau."

117.   Osofsky, Gilbert.   The Burden of Race.   New York:   Harper & Row,
1967.

> This book includes letters written by Northerners which describe
> their experiences in teaching Southern blacks.   Some of the students
> included black adults as the following account from Staunton,
> Virginia, exemplifies:
>
> "Among our scholars is one class of adults, who are taking two or
> three months rest from labor, for the purpose of getting an
> education.   It is really painful to see them toiling so faithfully
> at their primers, knowing, as we do, that, with all their earnest-
> ness, they will never see more than a glimmer of the light that has
> been shut out from them, and it is a relief to turn from them to
> the children who stride from alphabet to primer, and from primer to
> reader, in a wonderfully short time."

118.   Parker, Marjorie H.   "The Educational Activities of the Freedmen's
Bureau."   Ph.D. dissertation, University of Chicago, 1951.

> While the title of this dissertation may lead the reader to conclude
> that this work only deals with the educational activities of the
> Freedmen's Bureau, in reality it is much more comprehensive.   It
> covers almost every aspect of the Bureau from its conceptualization
> to its demise in 1872.
>
> Initially, the Bureau was to assist in the most urgent needs of the
> freedmen and refugees including problems concerning land, health
> care, transportation, marriage, labor, justice and claims.   There
> were no provisions for education; however, once the most urgent
> needs of blacks were satisfied, the efforts of the Bureau increasingly
> centered upon educational activities among the freedmen.   Many
> benevolent organizations, mainly from the North and a few from the
> South, joined forces with the Bureau to make provisions for black
> education, including many educational programs for adults.   In
> addition to efforts to establish educational programs for blacks,
> the Bureau served as a central coordinator of education for all
> benevolent organizations.

119.   Perkins, Francis B.   "Two Years With a Colored Regiment."   New
England Magazine, 17:533-543 (January, 1898).

> This article is written by the wife of a colonel in the Civil War.
> She describes her experience in assisting Negro soldiers in learning
> the rudiments of education.   She reports that instruction was also
> provided by chaplains and officers and that Negroes spent most of
> their free time making use of a speller, primer or a Testament.

120.   Porter, Berry.   "The History of Negro Education in Louisana."
Louisiana Historical Quarterly, 25:728-821 (July, 1942).

> Writing in the standard pre-World War II tradition, Porter indicts
> the Reconstruction experiments for corruption, fraud and for being
> a misguided integration experiment.   She focuses on the educational
> activities of the Jeanes teachers, Negro Farm Demonstration agents
> and the early efforts of the Ursuline Nuns in black and Indian

women's education. The emphasis throughout is on the themes of
education and self-help without analyzing the limitations of these
efforts in a racist society.

121. Quarles, Benjamin. Lincoln and the Negroes. New York: Oxford
University Press, 1962.

Quarles explores the relationship between President Abraham Lincoln
and the Negroes. While some were critical, others considered
Lincoln to be a friend to the Negro. One of his major contributions
was his signing of the bill on March 3, 1865, creating the Bureau
of Refugees, Freedmen, and Abandoned Lands. The Freedmen's Bureau
became one of the most noted Federal agencies with part of its
energies expended in the promotion of black education.

122. _____. The Negro in the Civil War. Boston: Little,
Brown and Co., 1953.

In his discussion of the Negroes' experiences during the Civil War,
the author discusses his status as a civilian and as a soldier in
the Union Army. He cites numerous educational opportunities
provided the Negro adult. Northern missionaries were perhaps most
instrumental in providing instructions.

123. Rabinowitz, Howard N. Race Relations in the Urban South, 1865-
1890. Urban Life in America Series. New York: Oxford University Press,
1971. Chapter 7.

Rabinowitz emphasizes the positive aspect of the Reconstruction Era
and underscores the negative impact of the Redeemer governments'
actions on black education. He notes the black adults' desire for
education as evidenced in the establishment of a night school in
Richmond, Virginia.

124. Ransom, Roger L., and Richard Sutch. One Kind of Freedom: The
Economic Consequences of Emancipation. Cambridge, London and New York:
Cambridge University Press, 1977.

The author's provocative study of slave literacy levels and
occupations challenges the notion that slavery was a good "school"
for slaves and prepared blacks for freedom. The authors argue that
it was not the anti-literacy laws so much as the slaveowners'
disinterest in slave literacy that explains antebellum practices.
Although some slaves had opportunity to "steal" literacy, this was
very limited. Furthermore, except for the blacksmiths and
carpenters, slaves were not trained, as a rule, in skilled trades
which required extensive training. The relatively small percentage
of ex-slaves in skilled trades in 1871 was not due so much to racism
after the Civil War as to the fact that slavery was not as good a
school as it has often been assumed.

125. Reimers, David M. White Protestantism and the Negro. New York:
Oxford University Press, 1965.

The Protestants were among the first promoters of Negro education
particularly during the Civil War years. Those cited by the

author as being most prominent include Northern Methodists, Baptists, Presbyterians, Episcopalians and Lutherans.

126. Richardson, Joe M. "Christian Abolitionism: The American Missionary Association and the Florida Negro." Journal of Negro Education, 40:35-44 (Winter, 1971).

Richardson highlights the efforts of the American Missionary Association in the education of the freedmen, and analyzes the relationship between the AMA and the Florida freedmen's thirst for learning. According to Richardson, the young and the old studied together, "grandparents and grandchildren thronged the crude schoolhouses--to secure 'the magic of reading and writing.'"

127. _____. A History of Fisk University, 1865-1946. University, Ala.: University of Alabama Press, 1980.

Richardson's first chapter provides a brief overview of the freedmens' thirst for and efforts in gaining literacy.

128. _____. "The Negro in Post Civil-War Tennessee: A Report by a Northern Missionary." Journal of Negro Education, 34:419-424 (Fall, 1965).

This article discusses the Negro educational activities conducted by Northern missionaries in Tennessee. Adults also were part of the educational endeavor as the following quotation illustrates:

". . . the child of seven and the child of seventy reading on the same page. . . . Reports of the young and elderly studying together were common throughout the South."

129. _____. The Negro in the Reconstruction of Florida, 1865-1877. Florida State University Studies No. 46. Tallahassee, Fl.: Florida State University Press, 1965. Chapter 9.

Richardson provides a succint account of the Freedmen's Bureau's efforts in black education up to 1870. He discusses the ex-slaves' thirst for literacy, the educational efforts of the Union Army, the establishment of plantation schools, the efforts to recruit white teachers and the establishment of teacher training institutions for blacks. Of special importance is Richardson's negative evaluation of plantation schools, enrolling both children and adults, arguing that they were established by planters in hopes of controlling the freedmen. Richardson's observation that black adult attendance declined after 1868 suggests perhaps that much of the activities in adult education was somewhat superficial with limited lasting results.

130. Shannon, Fred A. The Organization and Administration of the Union Army, 1861-1865. Cleveland: Arthur H. Clark Co., 1928.

Over 200,000 Negroes eventually enlisted in the Union Army. The Army itself chose to deal with the literacy problems of its Negro soldiers and civilians who took shelter behind Union lines. This

book briefly describes the efforts of the Army to educate the
Afro-American.

131.  Schweninger, Loren.  "The American Missionary Association and
Northern Philanthropy in Reconstruction Alabama."  Alabama Historical
Quarterly, 32:129-156 (Fall, 1970).

Schweninger provides a positive evaluation of Northern philanthropic
efforts, especially the American Missionary Society's in promoting
education including black adult education, and instilling the
notion of self-help within the black community.

132.  Smallwood, James M.  "Early Freedom Schools:  Black Self-Help and
Education in Reconstruction--Texas, A Case Study."  Negro History
Bulletin, 41:790-793 (January-February, 1978).

Smallwood describes the Texas blacks' zeal for literacy and highlights the black community's efforts in self-education, establishment of schools, the purchasing of printed materials and recruitment
of black teachers.

133.  Smith, Thomas H.  "Ohio Quakers and the Mississippi Freedmen--'A
Field to Labor.'"  Ohio History, 78:159-171 (Summer, 1969).

Smith describes the activities of and explores the conservative
philosophy underlying the Quakers' educational efforts among the
freedmen at Jackson, Mississippi.  Included in the article is a
description of the work among adults including the establishment of
an industrial school emphasing classes in garment making and the
sale of clothing for women.

134.  Swint, Henry L.  The Northern Teacher in the South, 1862-1870.
Nashville:  Vanderbilt University Press, 1941.

This is a study of the Northern schoolmarms who came South to teach
the freedmen during the period 1862-1870.  The study examines their
motives for participation, their attitude toward the existing
condition and their reaction to their experiences.  In the main, the
Northern teacher is viewed negatively.

Much of the financial support for the education was provided by the
Freedmen's Bureau and benevolent societies and associations in
America and abroad.  During the period studied, the author estimates
that more than $5,000,000 was spent on Negro education in the South.

135.  Taylor, Alrutheus A.  The Negro in Tennessee, 1865-1880.
Washington, D.C.:  The Associated Publishers, Inc., 1941.

Chapter 9 is entitled "Education in the Common Branches."  The
author reports that the Union Army, under the direction of the Army
chaplain, was instrumental in rallying support for Negro education.
Assistance was also solicited and obtained from The Western
Freedmen's Aid Commission.  Schools were established throughout
Tennessee for freedmen, including the black adults.  The values
promoted in these schools are highlighted in the following
quotation:

".  .  . the old and young showed an eager desire for education .  .  .
women and girls are taught to sew neatly .  .  . they are acquiring
habits of neatness, industry and economy; they are imbibing notions
of self-reliance and self-government; and they are being inspired
with respect for marriage, the family and home. .  .  . Wherever
properly cared for, they soon become qualified for the privileges
and responsibilities of freedom."

136.  _____.  The Negro in the Reconstruction of Virginia.
Washington, D.C.:  The Association for the Study of Negro Life and
History, 1926.

In Chapter 8, "Solving the Problem of Education," Taylor underscores
the Virginia freedmen's thirst for education and discusses the
contributions of benevolent organizations in educating the freedmen.
Most noteable was the American Missionary Association.  It
established day and night schools for Negroes of all ages utilizing
any available facilities including churches, warehouses, barns,
abandoned military quarters and the outdoors.  The Freedmen's
Bureau eventually took control of Negro education in the state.

137.  Taylor, Susie King.  Reminiscence of My Life in Camp.  Reprint.
New York:  Arno Press, 1968.

Included in the Reminiscences are a few references to Taylor's work
in teaching the soldiers in Company E to read and write and opening
a night school for adults in Savannah in 1867 and 1868.

138.  Tomlinson, Everett T.  A Leader of Freedmen.  Philadelphia:
American Sunday School Union, 1917.

Tomlinson provides a brief, laudatory account of the life of Samuel
Chapman Armstrong, first principal of Hampton Institute.  As an
agent of the Freedmen's Bureau, he was responsible for managing the
affairs of thousands of emancipated slaves in Virginia. Armstrong is
characterized as a Christian gentleman, a man of vision, a man of
integrity, a loyal soldier and a leader of the freedmen.  Tomlinson
depicts Armstrong as being especially sensitive to the freedmen's
educational needs, and he cites the many educational programs which
he initiated to meet their needs.

139.  Walker, Clarence E.  A Rock in a Weary Land:  The African
Methodist Episcopal Church during the Civil War and Reconstruction.
Baton Rouge and London:  Louisiana State University Press, 1982.

Walker argues that the AME Church's mission to the slaves and
freedmen was a mission to elevate the race.  Prior to the Civil War,
AME leaders assumed that anti-black prejudice was a product of the
black's lowly status rather than his color or race.  Consequently,
the AME leadership promoted self-improvement, education and moral
uplift.  Education was promoted not only for the ministers but for
the black laity as well.  Their analysis proved to be naive and
incorrect.  Walker analyzes the attempts and failures of the AME
Church to solve the problem of race prejudice through self-
improvement.

140. Wesley, Charles H., and Patricia W. Romero, International Library of Negro Life and History--Negro Americans in the Civil War. New York: Publishers Company, Inc., 1967.

The section entitled "Education in the Union Army" vividly depicts the educational efforts of the Union Army regarding the Negro.

"The Union Army became a type of school for the freedmen who had joined as soldiers and for those who had flocked into its lines from enslaved conditions. . . ."

"A variety of educational programs was carried out for colored soldiers. . . . Some of the more intelligent Union officers were the responsible agents in the schools for soldiers and freedmen."

". . . Many colored chaplains divided their time between preaching, aiding the sick and teaching."

141. West, Earl H. "The Harris Brothers: Black Northern Teachers in the Reconstruction South." Journal of Negro Education, 48:126-138 (Spring, 1979).

This article portrays the saga of three Negro brothers who joined the trek South to offer their assistance as teachers of freedmen. They traveled throughout the South establishing day, evening and Sabbath schools for the young and old.

142. Wiley, Bell I. Southern Negroes, 1861-1865. New York: Rinehart & Company Inc., 1938.

The educational system in the New Orleans vicinity was much more developed than in some of the remote areas and indeed some of the larger cities of the South. According to Wiley, "There were over 2,000 adults receiving instruction in high schools and Sunday schools under the Board of Education for Freedmen."

143. Williamson, Joel. After Slavery: The Negro in South Carolina During Reconstruction, 1861-1877. Chapel Hill, N.C.: University of North Carolina Press, 1965.

The author briefly describes what the Union Army meant to the Negro soldier educationally. Besides learning to be a good soldier, many Negro soldiers learned the rudiments of education, principles of investment and thrift and generally how to face the perils of freedom. This book also includes a chapter entitled "Education: Progress and Poverty," analyzing the manumitted's struggle for intellectual enlightenment in South Carolina during Reconstruction.

# 3
# SEPARATE BUT EQUAL, 1880–1930

144. Anderson, James D. "The Hampton Model of Normal School Industrial Education, 1868-1900." In Vincent P. Anderson and James D. Anderson, eds. New Perspectives on Black Educational History. Boston: G. K. Hall, 1978. Pp. 61-96.

In his revisionist study of Hampton Normal and Agricultural Institute, Anderson presents the thesis that the importance of the Hampton model lay not so much in its promotion of technical or agricultural training, but rather in its attempt "to train a cadre of conservative black teachers who were expected to help adjust the Afro-American minority to a subordinate role in the Southern political economy." He argues that Hampton's founder, Samuel Armstrong, assumed that the black race was "mentally capable but morally feeble" and as such should be stripped of the franchise. Armstrong viewed Northern capital and cheap black labor as being indispensible for Southern reconstruction. The Hampton model, encompassing its academic program, a manual labor system, and a strict discipline routine was designed for the creation of a black teacher force dedicated to transmitting Hampton's notions concerning the subordinate role of the black to the Afro-American working class.

145. Bellamy, Donnie D. "Henry Alexander Hunts' Crusade for Quality Public Education of Black Georgians." The Negro Educational Review, 28:85-94 (April, 1977).

Bellamy provides an analysis of Henry Alexander Hunts' efforts to promote improved education in the public sector in Georgia, 1904-1933, and of his efforts in educating the adults on the need for concerted action for improving education for blacks. Included in the article is a discussion of the funding and the goals of the "Georgia Association for the Advancement of Education Among Negroes."

146. Bettye, Bess. "Black Newspapers: Neglected Source for the New South." Negro Historical Bulletin, 43:60-62 (July, Aug., Sept., 1980).

The article provides a brief analysis of six influential black editors in the late nineteenth century and of their importance to the education of the black community. Bettye argues that the editors' writings ranged from myth making to hard-nosed reality, and that the editors were both influenced by and influenced in turn the black community.

147. Brawley, Benjamin. A Short History of the American Negro. New York: The Macmillan Co., 1939.

Briefly depicted in this short historical treatise of the American Negro is an account of the significant contribution of Booker T. Washington and George Washington Carver toward educating the black adult population in Tuskegee and throughout Alabama. Washington and Carver impressed upon the black masses the importance of education, and the importance for blacks to improve their living conditions and the quality of their lives.

These educators instituted numerous programs and projects aimed at enlightening black adults including: (1) Annual Negro Conferences, (2) Monthly Farmers' Institutes, (3) Agriculture Short Courses, (4) Farm Demonstration Workshops, (5) A Town Night School, (6) County Institutes, (7) A Ministers' Night School, (8) Mothers' Meetings, (9) State and County Fairs and (10) Special Conferences on the Negro as a World Problem.

148. Brown, Roscoe C. "The National Negro Health Week Movement." Journal of Negro Education, 6:553-564 (July, 1937).

The focus of this article is on one aspect of the health education movement, the National Negro Health Week. Brown traces the National Negro Health Week movement from its origin as a one-week effort at Tuskegee Institute, providing practical suggestions to local committees for improving local health conditions and stimulating local self-help efforts in sanitation, hygiene and clinical services, to its expansion as an all-year movement at Howard University. The article includes a case study of one community's participation in the movement. Although useful as a descriptive account of the National Negro Health Week movement, the article fails to provide an adequate analysis of the limitation of the self-help and self-reliant ideology, characteristic of the movement and of much of black adult education generally.

149. Butler, Jon. "Communities and Congrgations: The Black Church in St. Paul, 1860-1900." Journal of Negro History, 56:118-134 (April, 1971).

Based on a study of the Pilgrim Baptist and St. James African Methodist Episcopal churches, Butler concludes that the black churches in St. Paul did not serve as true "community" institutions. With their emphasis on education and respectability, the black churches in St. Paul served a selective clientele. Butler describes the extensive educational programs undertaken through the Sunday Schools, sewing circles, literary societies as well as German language courses offered by the St. James AME Church for members

who worked as laborers and house servants. (Butler has provided an
excellent discussion on the importance of the black church in adult
education.)

150.   Campbell, Thomas M.   The Moveable School Goes to the Negro Farmer
Tuskegee:  Tuskegee Institute Press, 1939.

The author, Thomas Monroe Campbell, was the first Negro extension
agent chosen by the Federal Government and the first to operate the
Moveable School at Tuskegee Institute.  His book serves somewhat of
a tribute to Booker T. Washington and George Washington Carver.
Both played significant roles in the operation and success of the
program.  The primary purpose of the program was to improve the
quality of life of Negroes in rural Alabama through a moveable
instruction program.

The purpose and result of this type adult education is outlined in
the book.  The impact of this program on this country and abroad is
also addressed.  Finally, the book discusses the future of Negroes
in rural life.  In the main, the book presents a non-critical,
laudatory account of the Tuskegee philosophy of education and self-
help.

151.   _____.   The School Comes to the Farm.   New York:
Longmans Green and Co., 1910.

Since its inception, Tuskegee Institute in Tuskegee, Alabama, was
involved in educating Negro adults throughout rural Alabama.
Conferences and institutes of various sorts were held on the college
campus for farmers, ministers and the general Negro public.  One of
the institution's most unique adult education projects was the
moveable school.  Instructional supplies were taken by a horse drawn
wagon to the constituents where demonstrations became a vital
component of the instructional strategy.  This book describes the
moveable school project in great detail.

152.   Carter, Purvis M.   "Robert Lloyd Smith and the Farmer's Improvement
Society, a Self-Help Movement in Texas."  Negro History Bulletin, 29:
175-177, 190 (Fall, 1966).

The author discusses the activities of R. L. Smith and the Farmer's
Improvement Society in the early twentieth century in promoting
racial identity and pride through cooperative action, and the
promotion of values of self-help, thrift, industriousness,
punctuality and wholesome family life.  Emphasis is given to the
Society's emphasis on the education of the rural black.  The tenor
of the whole article is clearly within the Booker T. Washington
tradition of self-help, thrift and industry.

153.   Cooley, Rossa B.   School Acres:  An Adventure in Rural Education.
New Haven:  Yale University Press, 1930.

This is an account of the Penn School Experiment on St. Helena
Island by one of its major participants in the twentieth century.
The emphasis throughout is on the attempt by the missionaries to use
Penn School as a vehicle for the education of the entire rural black

community. Most useful for the study of adult education is Part IV, "The Grown Folks Came to School." This section provides an excellent description of the methodology utilized in making the Penn School experiment an "adventure in adult education." Included here are descriptions of community classes in serving, knitting, basketry, Bible, hygiene, home nursing; the organization of homemakers clubs; the role of the Penn School nurse in offering classes for midwives; and, the School's attempt to promote scientific farming. School Acres serves as a useful source for historians seeking to understand the values, attitudes and goals of the Northern missionaries as well as a case study in rural, black community education.

154. Fortune, T. Thomas. Black and White: Land, Labor and Politics in the South. New York: Fords, Howard, & Humbert, 1884.

Fortune addresses the black experience in the late nineteenth century. He highlights the educational activities of the churches in promoting education for the Southern black.

155. Franklin, Vincent P. "In Pursuit of Freedom: The Educational Activities of Black Social Organizations in Philadelphia, 1900-1930." In Vincent P. Franklin and James Anderson, eds. New Perspectives on Black Educational History. Boston: G. K. Hall, 1978. pp. 113-128.

Franklin provides an excellent case study of "community-wide educational activities of black social organizations and institutions" in a twentieth-century urban community. Included in the analysis are the educational activities provided through lectures, conferences, historical organizations which emphasized education in the black heritage; educational activities of black social, religious and fraternal institutions emphasizing education for individual and community development; and activities of black social organizations emphasizing education for black social and political advancement. Franklin argues that both race and status conscious organizations were active in promoting educational activities which were not aimed primarily at the middle class but focused on issues affecting all the blacks in Philadelphia and "were an important part of the social environment of blacks in urban America."

Franklin's essay is one of the few studies, to date, that deal adequately with the education of the urban black community during and following the large in-migration of Southern blacks to Northern cities after 1916. Franklin moves beyond the school house to literary societies, black historical societies, religious institutions including the YMCA and YWCA, black women's groups and the NAACP to describe and analyze their efforts in educating the black community, including the black adult. His essay serves as a reminder that one needs to move beyond the day school when seeking to understand the education of a minority group.

156. Gardner, Booker T. "The Educational Contributions of Booker T. Washington." Journal of Negro Education, 14:502-518 (Fall, 1975).

At Tuskegee Institute, Booker T. Washington put together one of the most effective extension programs that could be found on any college campus in America. His constituents were rural Negro adults, although some whites were served. This article briefly discusses this project.

157. Gerber, David A. Black Ohio and the Color Line, 1869-1915. Urbana, Ill.: University of Illinois Press, 1976.

Gerber analyzes the upper- and middle-class bias both in membership of and activities promoted by Ohio black religious, fraternal and social institutions in the late nineteenth century. Included in his discussion are activities of urban black churches, Masons and women's clubs as well as groups such as the YMCA and the Colored Women's League. The latter were more responsive in their programs to the needs of the poor. Gerber notes that it was the younger black leadership which was both more responsive to the needs of the poor and advocated the establishment of racially exclusive institutions.

158. Harlan, Louis R. Booker T. Washington: The Making of a Black Leader, 1856-1901. New York: Oxford University Press, 1972.

Harlan includes a brief but insightful analysis of the Tuskegee Negro Conference for farmers established by Booker T. Washington in 1902. Focusing on the Tuskegee themes of racial accommodation, thrift, rural self-help and crop diversification, the conferences served as a showcase for the Tuskegee concept and won the approval of white Southerners.

159. Harley, Sharon. "Beyond the Classroom: The Organizational Lives of Black Female Educators in the District of Columbia." Journal of Negro Education, 51:254-265 (Summer, 1982).

Harley explores a movement largely overlooked by social historians in American history, the black "social settlement" movement in the early twentieth century. Her work is primarily descriptive in nature. Although the black female educators were clearly drawn from the middle class, Harley does not explore adequately the extent to which the black social settlement movement was able to effectively reach the working class, black female.

160. Harris, Nelson H. "In-Service Teacher Training Facilities of North Carolina Negro Institutions." Journal of Negro Education, 9:44-50 (January, 1940).

Harris describes efforts by North Carolina institutions during the 1920's and 1930's to provide in-service training for teachers, many of whom had not graduated from high school. Included were extension programs, summer school courses in county schools and correspondence courses.

161. Hines, Linda E. O. "Background to Fame: The Career of George Washington Carver, 1896-1916." Ph.D. dissertation, Auburn University, 1976.

The primary focus of this dissertation is on a twenty-year period of Carver's professional life at Tuskegee Institute in Tuskegee,

Alabama. One of the chapters is devoted exclusively to Carver's extension activities. A major portion of his efforts in extension work was directed toward the improvement of the living conditions of Negroes in rural Alabama. His greatest achievements in this regard resulted from his scientific experiments. He eagerly shared his discoveries with his people through various publications, the Tuskegee Farmers' Conference, the Macon County Fair, the Tuskegee Experiment Station and the Moveable School. He offered advice on such areas as food preservation, farming, cattle production, soil conservation, cleanliness and health care.

162. Jackson, Luther P. "The Work of the Association and the People." Journal of Negro History, 20:385-396 (October, 1935).

This article provides an assessment of the impact of the Association for the Study of Negro Life and History upon the people during its first twenty years of existence, especially in instilling pride in the Afro-American heritage through the Journal of Negro History, the establishment of clubs, speaking engagements of Carter Woodson and through the establishment of Negro History Week.

163. Jacoway, Elizabeth. Yankee Missionaries in the South: The Penn School Experiment. Baton Rouge and London: Louisiana State University Press, 1980.

Yankee Missionaries is a study primarily of two Northern missionaries, Rossa Belle Cooley and Grace Bigelow House, and of the Penn School trustees' goals and activities in the Penn School Experiment on St. Helena Island after 1900. A major objective of the Penn School Experiment was to utilize "industrial" education, broadly defined, for the revitalization of the rural black Southern community. Within this context adult education played an important role. Jacoway provides an excellent description of adult education activities, an integral part of the teachers' attempts to transform Penn School into a community school. Mention is made of education in agriculture, homemaking, health and hygiene through the use of farm and home demonstrations, farmers' fairs, adult classes, homemaker's clubs, classes for midwives and through the implementation of the All-Year School. Undergirding the All-Year School were the assumptions that the community school be used as a classroom and the children could be utilized as vehicles for educating black adults. (Yankee Missionaries is an excellent study, based on solid research.)

164. James, Felix. "The Tuskegee Institute Movable School, 1906-1923." Agricultural History, 45:201-209 (July, 1971).

The Tuskegee Institute Movable School provided demonstration and instruction in agriculture and homemaking. James explores the Tuskegee philosophy of self-help and land ownership and describes the work of Thomas M. Campbell, the first black Demonstration Agent in the U.S. Department of Agriculture, and the extensive educational activities of the "Booker T. Washington Agriculture School on Wheels." Highly laudatory and primarily descriptive in nature, the article provides a useful perspective on the public or stated goals of black adult education built on the Tuskegee Philosophy.

165. Jones, Beverly W. "Mary Church Terrell and the National Association of Colored Women, 1896 to 1901." Journal of Negro History, 67:20-33 (Spring, 1982).

Jones analyzes Mary Church Terrell's efforts in creating the National Association of Colored Women (NACW), and describes Terrell's and NACW's efforts in organizing kindergartens, nurseries, mother's clubs and homes for girls, the aged and the infirm. Jones explores both the conservativism and radicalism evident within NACW. As a middle-class dominated organization, emphasizing the uplift of the black home and the black masses, it was conservative in outlook. But as a "nationalized effort exclusively created and controlled by black women" and serving as a laboratory for the training of black women in leadership skills it was a radical movement.

166. Lamon, Lester. Black Tennesseans: 1900-1930. Knoxville, University of Tennessee Press, 1977.

Lamon's social history of black Tennesseans includes several excellent sections which have special relevance for the study of adult education. One section is the chapter "On the Agricultural Margin" where Lamon discusses the establishment of the West Tennessee Farmer's Institute, the organization of the Farmers Institute in Nashville, and the appoinment--albeit belatedly--of black farm agents, and the formation of black county fairs. Another section "Progressivism--for Whites Only?" disputes the notion that a progressive spirit was not evident within the black middle class. It discusses the work of black middle-class dominated organizations including the Negro newspapers, the Nashville Negro Board of Trade, the black women's club, the YMCA, homemaker clubs, ministerial alliances and educational associations. Anchored in the Booker T. Washington concept of self-help, these groups sought to improve the image of the Negro race in the eyes of white society.

167. Lerner, Gerda. "Early Community Work of Black Club Women." Journal of Negro History, 59:158-167 (April, 1974).

Lerner argues that "contrary to widely held myths, black communities have a continuous record of self-help, institution-building and strong organization to which black women have made continuous contributions." Her article focuses on the activities of black club women at Tuskegee, in New York, Washington, D.C., and Atlanta and describes their extensive efforts in promoting social and recreational programs, literary discussions, self-study circles, mother's meetings, classes in Negro history, religious activities and hygiene and anti-discrimination drives. Although led by middle-class women, Lerner argues that the clubs were successful in bridging the class barriers and were concerned with the problems of the poor black families.

168. Lindsay, I. B. "Adult Education Programs for Negroes in Settlement Houses." Journal of Negro Education, 14:347-352 (Summer, 1945).

Lindsay utilizes selected settlement houses to demonstrate their potential in becoming instruments of adult education. Settlement houses in the North stressed educational activities designed to help the black in becoming more adequately socially adjusted. Negro settlement houses stressed not only vocational training and cultural programs but also, like the National Federation of Settlements during World War II, education in racial understanding.

169. Locke, Alain. "Negro Education Bids for Poor." Survey Graphic, 54:567 (September, 1925).

In this article the author is critical of the American system for the obvious disparity between educational opportunities available to Negroes and whites. He addresses nearly all aspects of education and concludes that no matter how it is viewed, Negroes receive disproportionately less. The article challenges the American public to face squarely the issue of Negro education.

170. Logan, Frenise A. The Negro in North Carolina, 1876-1894. Chapel Hill, N.C.: University of North Carolina Press, 1964.

Negro adults in North Carolina were provided educational opportunities as early as the Colonial period. The religious sects most aggressive in promoting Negro education were the Anglican Church, Episcopalians, Presbyterians, Methodists and especially the Quakers. The author highlights the activities of the religious groups as well as the Negro press in educating the black adult.

171. Martorella, Peter H. "The Negroes' Role in American History: George Washington Carver--A Case Study." Social Studies, 60:318-325 (December, 1969).

While historians have noted George Washington Carver's scientific discoveries, they have largely overlooked his contribution as an adult educator. In addition to highlighting Carver's career as a scientist, Martorella credits Carver with much of Tuskegee Institute's educational programs for the black adults. Carver wrote numerous pamphlets for adults and put on demonstrations highlighting his scientific discoveries throughout rural Alabama.

172. McGee, Leo. "George Washington Carver: Agricultural Scientist and Extension Worker." Farm and Home Bulletin, Tennessee State University (November, 1976). P. 1.

George Washington Carver is best known for his scientific discoveries as a faculty member at Tuskegee Institute. One of his major goals was to help his people improve the quality of their lives. This article describes how Carver, through his extension work, shared his scientific knowledge with black adults throughout rural Alabama.

173. McPherson, James M. The Abolitionist Legacy. Princeton, N.J.: Princeton University Press, 1975.

McPherson challenges the assumption that the abolitionists lost their concern for equality after the Reconstruction era. Focusing

on the American Missionary Association schools rather than on
Tuskegee and Hampton Institutes, McPherson argues that the
abolitionists in these institutions remained committed to the
principle of eventual racial equality. They assumed, however, that
the road to equality would only be realized if the ex-slaves became
ebony Puritans. Chapter 4, "Time, Education, and Bootstraps," is
especially useful for a study of the abolitionists' values as
exemplified in the educational programs.

174. Meier, August. Negro Thought in America, 1880-1915. Ann Arbor:
The University of Michigan Press, 1963.

Meier highlights several aspects which have relevance for the study
of the education of the black adult. One is his discussion of
entrepreneurialship which was prominent in the black community.
Much of the education Negro adults obtained during this period came
about as a result of their own efforts. From the late 1880's there
was a remarkable development of Negro businesses including banks,
insurance companies, undertakers and retail stores. This was
significant in that there was a demise of white patronization of
Negro barbers, tailors, caters, blacksmiths and other artisans.
Also important is Meier's discussion of the thoughts and educational
philosophies of Booker T. Washington and W. E. B. DuBois.

175. Moorland, J. E. "The Young Man's Christian Association Among
Negroes." Journal of Negro History, 9:127-138 (January, 1924).

Moorland's article, written in the Booker T. Washington spirit of
racial accommodation, traces the work of the YMCA from the
appointment in 1888 of William A. Hutton as the first salaried
black employee to work among the blacks to the early twentieth
century. The work, although highly laudatory when it comes to
trumpeting the goodwill of Southern whites and blacks in the
movement, does provide useful background information in the early
history of the YMCA's work among blacks, especially in Chicago.

176. Morton, Robert R. "Hampton, Tuskegee and Points North." Survey
Graphic, 54:15-18 (April, 1925).

This article is primarily centered on the industrial education
thrust at Tuskegee Institute under the leadership of Booker T.
Washington. It also describes Washington's goal of reaching parents
of his college students.

". . . While the boys and girls were being taught in the class
rooms, the fathers and mothers were being reached in the field and
in the home; education was carried to them in simple direct terms
made plain by demonstrations. . . ."

177. Neverdon-Morton, Cynthia. "Self-Help Programs as Educative
Activities of Black Women in the South, 1895-1915: Focus on Four Key
Areas." Journal of Negro Education, 51:207-221 (Summer, 1982).

This article focuses on self-help programs in Tuskegee, Hampton,
Atlanta and Baltimore sponsored by black women's groups through which
the women defined "their role and responsibility in providing

self-help and social service programs for uplifting of the race."
Programs ranged from efforts to improve health and sanitation
conditions in Atlanta and Baltimore to holding mother's meetings and
establishing a night school offering courses in industrial training,
cooking and academic subjects in the Tuskegee area.  What is not
analyzed sufficiently is the middle-class orientation of these
groups, nor to what extent each group was founded on the Booker T.
Washington philosophy of self-reliance, moral uplift and gradualism.

178.   Newby, I. A.   Black Carolinians:  A History of Blacks in South
Carolina from 1865 to 1968.   Columbia, S.C.:  University of South
Carolina Press, 1973.

   One useful section for the study of the education of the black
   adult is Newby's discussion of the black church in the era of white
   supremacy.  Newby notes the importance of the black church in
   leadership training as well as its emphasis on self-help, moral
   living and obedience to the law.

179.   Osofsky, Gilbert.   The Making of a Ghetto:  Negro New York, 1890-
1930.   Second edition, New York:  Harper Torchbooks, 1971.

   The author analyzes the efforts of religious organizations, social
   settlement workers, black improvement organizations and public
   health organizations in Harlem in the early twentieth century.  Most
   important is the author's discussion of reform and educational
   efforts of the urban progressives, both black and white, during the
   first decade of the twentieth century.

   Osofsky argues that as the pace of in-migration of blacks
   accelerated, the walls of segregation were raised.  The in-migration
   of blacks prodded churches into going beyond their traditional
   religious emphasis to developing educational activities in sewing,
   cooking, music and providing lectures--activities which were aimed
   at lower as well as middle-class blacks.  In addition the YMCA,
   the Colored Women's Club movement and the Settlement houses promoted
   a variety of self-help activities for black adults.  These clubs,
   catering to specific groupings, reflected the increasing social
   stratification within the segregated black community.

180.   Robbins, Gerald.   "Rossa B. Cooley and Penn School:  Social
Dynamo in Negro Rural Subculture, 1901-1930."   Journal of Negro
Education, 33:43-51 (Winter, 1964).

   Penn School, founded in 1862 and located at St. Helena Island, South
   Carolina, was one of the first Negro schools established in the
   South during the Civil War.  This article describes the school during
   Miss Cooley's lengthy tenure.  The emphasis on adult education is
   highlighted in the following quotation:

   ". . . The principals urged parents to come to the classes and, if
   they could not, the teachers persuaded the children to teach their
   elders what they had learned. . . ."

181. Scott, Emmett J. Negro Migration During the War. Preliminary Economic Studies of the War, No. 16. New York: Oxford University Press, 1920. Chapters 9 & 13.

Chapters 9 and 13 include discussions of efforts by black urban organizations and institutions in the North to provide relief and education for the in-migrants from the South. Most important is Chapter 9 where Scott describes the work of the Negro Welfare Association of Cleveland and the National League on Urban Conditions in acting as clearing houses in dealing with problems of and in disseminating information useful for blacks.

182. Sherer, Robert G. Subordination or Liberation? The Development and Conflicting Theories of Black Education in Nineteenth Century Alabama. University, Ala.: University of Alabama Press, 1977.

Sherer provides a critical assessment of the limitations of industrial training in serving as an instrument of liberation for blacks. He analyzes Booker T. Washington's concept of Tuskegee as an institution serving all of Alabama's black population including the formation of a Savings Bank Department, the organization of the Southern Improvement Company, the establishment of the Phelps Hall Bible Training School for rural ministers and the Negro Farmer's and Worker's Conferences and the participation of Tuskegee faculty and students in local churches and temperance societies. In the end Washington is depicted as being more successful in helping his institution than in elevating his race.

183. Spear, Allan H. Black Chicago: The Making of a Negro Ghetto, 1890-1920. Chicago and London: University of Chicago Press, 1967.

Spear analyzes the formation of a black ghetto in Chicago and examines the forces which brought about the development of a segregated community. He also examines the impact of the immigration of Southern blacks during World War I upon the ghetto. Spear's study makes clear that the in-migration did not create the ghetto, it merely accelerated a process of segregation which was already in process.

Two chapters have special relevance for the study of adult education. The focus of Chapter 5 is on the response of black leaders prior to World War I to discrimination by white institutions including the establishment of a wide range of Negro operated community services. Included are descriptions of educational activities promoted by selected churches, the YMCA, the Colored Women's Club movement and the Settlement House. The focus in Chapter 9 is on the impact of migration on black community life. Of special importance here is the discussion of the Chicago Urban League, the YMCA, the YWCA and the black newspaper.

184. Thrasher, Max Bennett. Tuskegee: Its Story and Its Work. Reprint. New York: Negro University Press, 1969.

Bennett provides a laudatory, noncritical account of Tuskegee written in the Up From Slavery tone with its emphasis on self-help self-reliance, cleanliness and morality. Despite its bias it does

provide useful material on Tuskegee's emphasis on adult education
and community outreach including chapters on the Bible School, the
establishment of adult evening schools by Tuskegee graduates, the
farmers' conferences, the workers' conferences and mother's meetings
and women's clubs.

185.  Tindall, George B.  South Carolina Negroes, 1877-1900.  Columbia,
S.C.:  University of South Carolina Press, 1952.

The author acknowledged that several other works had been published
which addressed various aspects of Negro life in the state of South
Carolina.  However, there was little coverage of post-Reconstruction
developments.  This book is an effort to fill that void.  Its
primary focus is post-Reconstruction developments in Negro life and
institutions and in race relations.  It addresses such subjects as
the Negro Church, Negroes in Politics, The Decline of the Republican
Party and The Migratory Urge.

186.  Washington, Booker T.  The Story of the Negro.  New York:  Peter
Smith, 1940.

The Church played a significant role in the educational lives of
Negro adults.  It was their spiritual and social livelihood; it was
their source of renewal and regeneration; it was their means of news
currency; and, it was their community institution where an informal
education could be obtained.  It could be one of the most underrated
educational resources.

In the chapter, "The Negro Preacher and the Negro Church,"
Washington discusses the Negro church's influence on the Negro
community.

187.  _____.  Up From Slavery.  An Autobiography.  School
Edition.  Cambridge, Mass.:  Houghton-Mifflin--The Riverside Press,
1928.

In his up-beat biography, extolling the virtues of self-help, moral
uplift and the gospel of work, Washington documents briefly the
ex-slave's thirst for education.  He is critical, however, of the
freedmen's naive view of education, assuming that it would quickly
elevate him culturally and free him from manual labor.

188.  _____.  Working With Hands:  Being a Sequel to 'Up From
Slavery' Covering the Author's Experiences in Industrial Training at
Tuskegee.  New York:  Doubleday, Page and Company, 1904.

Chapters 10 and 11 provide an account of Booker T. Washington's
gospel of work, thrift, self-help, cleanliness and moral uplift as
it applied to community and adult education.  The work presents the
"public image" of Tuskegee's industrial and community education.
Chapter 10 describes the educational activities for mothers,
including Mrs. Washington's Women's meetings, the emphasis on home
beautification, proper dress and appropriate female behavior and
the organization of an adult night school, a Sunday School and a
Mothers Union on the settlement established near Tuskegee.

Chapter 11 focuses on adult education for farmers, with special emphasis on the Annual Tuskegee Negroes Conference. The conservative philosophy of gradualism and self-help permeates the discussion throughout this chapter.

189. Wolfe, Deborah. "Booker T. Washington: An Educator for All Ages." Phi Delta Kappan, 63:205 (November, 1981).

This article analyzes various aspects of Booker T. Washington's philosophy of education. Wolfe argues that Washington's contributions to the theory and practice of education trancend his time and remain relevant for the education enterprise, including adult education, today.

190. Woofter, Thomas J. Southern Race Progress. Washington, D.C.: Public Affairs Press, 1957.

This book provides a brief description of the educational activities for the Negro in St. Helena Island, South Carolina. One of the most noted attempts to educate Negro adults took place here.

191. Wright, George C. "Blacks in Louisville, Kentucky." Ph.D. dissertation, Duke University, 1977.

This is a study of the black leaders in Louisville, Kentucky, 1890–1930. Attention is devoted to their influence on various aspects of black life in the city including employment, business, social life and education.

# 4
# MODERN ERA, 1930–PRESENT

192. Aptheker, Herbert. "Literacy, The Negro and World War II."
Journal of Negro Education, 15:595-602 (Fall, 1946).

Aptheker provides an analysis of the reason for and a description of
instructional programs and Special Training Units established by the
military in 1943. Although set up in the Jim Crow pattern of
separate classes for blacks, the program demonstrated that where
blacks and whites were exposed to similar programs under similar
conditions, black's performance was comparable to that of the
white's.

193. Atkins, James A. "The Participation of Negroes in Pre-School and
Adult Education Programs." Journal of Negro Education, 7:345-346 (July,
1938).

Atkins describes aims and objectives of and blacks' participation
in adult education programs established by the Federal Emergency
Relief Administration. Although programs were expanded to include
general education and vocational training for unemployed adults,
including the physically handicapped, the main focus of black adult
education remained illiteracy training.

194. Bailey, Ronald W. Black Business Enterprise. New York: Basic
Books, Inc., 1971.

In this book the author contends that education is crucial if blacks
are to effectively compete in the business enterprise. He points
out that the lack of education has plagued this group since the
Colonial era.

195. Barnwell, F. Rivers. "Health Education of Negroes Provided by
Press, Radio and Theatre." Journal of Negro Education, 6:565-571 (July,
1937).

The article includes a description of health education activities by
radio, theatre, selected black newspapers, magazines and in films.

196. Bass, Floyd L. "Impact of the Black Experience on Attitudes Toward Continuing Education." Adult Education, 22:207-217 (Spring, 1972).

This study was designed to determine the attitudes of urban blacks toward continuing education. The number of adults in the research sample was 222. Bass concludes that blacks are somewhat skeptical of continuing education in that they have not experienced equitable participation in programs sponsored by universities, business enterprises, industrial organizations or other agencies involved in continuing education.

197. Blackwell, Gordon W. "Evaluation of Present Programs of Adult Education for Negroes." Journal of Negro Education, 14:443-452 (Summer, 1945).

Blackwell provides a useful summary of what was being done by different groups and organizations in five categories of adult education. He concludes: remedial education including literacy training is declining in importance, somewhat prematurely, health and nutrition education have received increased attention during World War II, cultural education still does not loom large in black adult education, vocational education is becoming increasingly important and social education will become very important. He also points out that the rural black population is still largely neglected when it comes to adult education, and that institutions such as the churches, schools, colleges and libraries which have the greatest potential for covering a broad area of population do not have adult education as their first mission, while other groups and organizations such as the Little Theater, NAACP and Urban League lack established channels for reaching the masses. This is an excellent concise overview of the state of black adult education at the end of World War II.

198. Bond, Max. "The Educational Program for Negroes in the TVA." Journal of Negro Education, 6:144-151 (April, 1937).

Bond, a supervisor of Negro training within the TVA, describes the educational activities and programs undertaken at Wheeler Dam, Alabama, and Pickwick Dam, Tennessee, as well as in other rural towns and communities. Included in the programs are training in the knowledge of tools and trade, basic courses in wiring, masonry, carpentry, auto mechanics, construction, elementary arithmetic and English, literacy training, homemaking, agriculture, general education, recreation and library service. Although providing a useful description of the broad range of activities, the article fails to analyze the TVA's discriminatory practices in training and placing blacks primarily in unskilled jobs such as custodians or laborers in reservoir clearance.

199. _____. "The Training Program of the Tennessee Valley Authority for Negroes." Journal of Negro Education, 7:383-389 (July, 1938).

The author describes the TVA training program for Negro workers and their families at Wheeler Dam and Wheeler Dam Reservoir Clearance

Area, Pickwick Dam and the Pickwick Dam Reservoir Clearance Area,
Guntersville Dam, Wilson Dam and in the Chattanooga area.  Programs
ranged from basic job training in automotive oiling and janitor
training to general education courses in the three R's, general
adult education, health education, homemaking and agriculture.  Of
special interest is Bond's description of the emergence of the
"Peoples College," run by workers and community members, offering
seminars dealing with problems of and progress in Negro life.
Although Bond recognizes problems due to race discrimination he
remains basically positive in outlook.

200.  Branson, Herman.  "The Training of Negroes for War Industries in
World War II."  Journal of Negro Education, 12:376-385 (Summer, 1943).

Branson describes the discriminatory nature but also improvement in
training programs for blacks from 1941 to 1943.  The greatest gain
for blacks after 1941 came in pre-employment rather than in on-the-
job training programs.  The latter was the key, however, for job
promotion.  Similarly few blacks were participating in Engineering,
Science and Management War Training Programs offered on college
campuses.  The author emphasizes the importance of governmental
programs designed to recruit and train black workers in a racist
society.

201.  Brazziel, William F.  "Manpower Training and the Negro Worker."
Journal of Negro Education, 35:83-89 (Winter, 1966).

This is a report on the Federal Manpower Development Training
project for the years 1962 to 1964, in which thousands of Negro
adults received job training and were placed in jobs.

202.  Brown, Francis J.  Educational Opportunities for Veterans.
Washington, D.C.:  Public Affairs Press, 1946.

Brown provides a thorough discussion of Public Law 346 passed by the
78th Congress and amended by Public Law 268, 79th Congress--the G.I.
Bill of Rights.  This law provides for education and training of all
veterans.  Thousands of Negro veterans have benefited from this
adult education program.

203.  Brown, Roscoe C.  "The Health Education Programs of Government and
Voluntary Agencies."  Journal of Negro Education, 18:377-387 (Summer,
1949).

Brown describes the increasing contribution of health and voluntary
agencies, both governmental and private, in providing health
services and promoting an increased awareness of health education
among blacks.  Included in the survey are Federal, state and local
governmental agencies; voluntary organizations; health activities of
interracial and black self-help organizations; and, the National
Negro Health Week Movement.  The article is basically descriptive
and fails to adequately deal with the  impact of racism except for a
brief comment that one notices a lessening in sensitivity to race
and self-interest which had previously hindered the health education
movement and presented an obstacle to gaining a clear understanding
of the health needs of the black community.

204. Bullock, Ralph W. "The Adult Education Programs of the YMCA Among Negroes." Journal of Negro Education, 14:385-389 (Summer, 1945).

The article includes a summary of adult education programs in twenty-three local YMCAs. Based on returns received from a questionnaire, the author provides a listing of how many black YMCAs provided what type of organized activity. Bullock concludes that although there is evidence of much activity it is not always linked to a constructive philosophy.

205. Bunche, Ralph J. "The Programs of Organizations Devoted to the Improvement of the Status of the American Negro." Journal of Negro Education, 8:539-550 (July, 1939).

Bunche provides a biting indictment of programs by organizations devoted to the improvement of black Americans and influential in the education of the black adult community. He argues that minority organizations and leadership "portray minority chauvinism in boldest relief." He cites eight major weaknesses inherent in the philosophy and structure of the black organizations including "(1) adherence to policies of escape, based upon racialism and nationalism; (2) lack of mass support among Negroes . . . ; (3) dependence upon white benefactors for finance; (4) reluctance to encourage the development of working-class psychology among Negroes and avoidance of class interpretations; (5) tendancy . . . to take their main ideological cues from white sympathizers; (6) lack of coherent, constructive programs; (7) lack of broad social perspective . . . ; and, (8) pursuit of policies of immediate relief and petty opportunism." Bunche analyzes both the Booker T. Washington and the W. E. B. DuBois school of thought and the organizations which sprang from these two movements. All are found wanting when it comes to leadership and broad social understanding.

206. Caliver, Ambrose. "Adult Education of Negroes: New Project Under Way." School Life, 29:26-28 (October, 1946).

A description of the origin and goals of a Carnegie Corporation financed project in black adult education. The purpose of the project was to train personnel and prepare materials for and stimulate interest in schools and communities in the education of black adults.

207. _____. "Progress Report on Adult Education of Negroes." School Life, 30:17 (January, 1948).

A brief report describing and evaluating a pilot program in black adult education.

208. _____. Vocational Education and Guidance of Negroes: Report of a Survey Conducted by the Office of Education. Westport, Conn.: Negro University Press, 1970 (Reprint, 1937).

The survey included approximately two hundred centers or institutions including, in the main, four-year high schools and colleges but also evening schools, proprietary schools and non-school agencies offering vocational education and guidance for blacks. Included in

the report is a discussion on agricultural education offered for
adult farmers in part-time and evening schools, Home Economics
education in evening schools and vocational education in trades and
industries offered in day and evening schools and in extension
centers. The high concentration of blacks in low skills level
courses and the small amount of Federal monies actually being
allotted for training blacks in trades and industries are noted.
Caliver does not question the importance of vocational education and
guidance for blacks but rather the efficacy of the programs as being
implemented in black institutions.

209. _____, and Theresa Wilkins. "Neglected Areas of Adult
Education Among Negroes: Teacher Training Programs." Journal of Negro
Education, 14:467-476 (Summer, 1945).

The authors survey the limited course offerings in black institutions
available for prospective teachers and leaders working with black
adults and present recommendations for improving teacher training
programs in adult education.

210. Campbell, J. Phil. "The Government's Farm Policies and the Negro
Farmer." Journal of Negro Education, 5:32-39 (January, 1936).

Campbell describes the establishment of "rural-industrial"
communities and their work-center program including the construction
and repair of work-center buildings, farm machinery repairs, food
processing and handicrafts, as well as other educational and cultural
activities such as community meetings, discussion groups, drama,
folk games and music.

211. Clayton, Ronald Keith. "Arthur Ernest Morgan and the Development
of an Adult Education Enterprise Within the Tennessee Valley Authority,
1933-1938." Ph.D. dissertation, Michigan State University, 1975.
Pp. 135-228.

The author argues that Arthur Morgan envisioned TVA serving as an
institution dedicated to the fullest development of the individual.
To accomplish this, Morgan launched a comprehensive program of adult
education based on his views of worthwhile societal values and a
philosophy of daily living. Although black adult education is not
emphasized, Clayton includes a description of the Negro program at
Muscle Shoals. The section dealing with the Negro program, as well
as the dissertation generally, is weak on social analysis. The
author presents a laudatory, non-critical analysis of Morgan's
educational philosophy disregarding the realities of class and race.
No mention is made of TVA's discriminatory practices in the hiring
and training of black adults.

212. Cooper, William A. "Adult Education Programs of Negro Colleges
and Universities." Journal of Negro Education, 14:307-311 (Summer,
1945).

This article contains a survey of offerings in, problems encountered
by, future plans of and recommendations for strengthening adult
education programs in black colleges.

213.  Cooper, William M.  "When X Day Comes for the Negro."  Adult
Education Journal, 3:60-61 (April, 1944).

    This article makes a strong plea for America to expand its efforts
    in Negro adult education.  The author's plea is precipitated by a
    perceived tension between the Negro and white races.

214.  Daniel, Walter G., and Carroll L. Miller.  "The Participation of
the Negro in the National Youth Administration Program."  Journal of
Negro Education, 7:357-365 (July, 1938).

    The authors discuss the participation of black youth of high school
    and college age and compare the ratio of blacks with whites in
    relief programs both as youth on relief and adults in administrative
    positions.  The authors note that although blacks were under-
    represented in NYA programs, the types of projects in which they
    were engaged did not reveal patterns of discrimination.

215.  De Costa, Frank A.  "The Education of Negroes in South Carolina."
Journal of Negro Education, 16:405-416 (Summer, 1947).

    This article contains a brief discussion on the provisions for and
    enrollment of black adults in educational programs, including public
    evening schools and community meetings.

216.  Dellefield, Calvin J.  "Aspirations of Low Socio-Economic Status
Adults and Implications for Adult Education."  Ed.D. dissertation,
University of California, Los Angeles, 1965.

    The purpose of this study was to determine the aspirations of a
    group of low socio-economic Negro adults in Los Angeles, California,
    and to draw implications for adult education.  The research sample
    consisted of 441 adults, 236 males and 205 females.  The interview
    technique was used for data collection.

    The study reveals that this group aspired to a higher quality of
    life for themselves and their children.  They desired comfort,
    happiness, prosperity and security much more so than education.
    Education was not viewed as being absolutely essential to the
    process of improving their status.

217.  Dockery, Christine.  "Recollections, Reflections, and Projections
of Selected Black Leaders in Adult Education."  Ph.D. dissertation,
Florida State University, 1976.

    This is a study of the philosophy of adult education of a selected
    group of five black leaders in the field of adult education,
    selected by a jury of peer adult educators.  Data were collected by
    the interview/oral history technique.

218.  Ekberg, Dennis, and Claude Ury.  "Education for What?:  A Report
on a M.D.T.A. Program."  Journal of Negro Education, 37:15-22 (Winter,
1968).

    This is a report on a Manpower Development and Training Act program
    conducted at Oakland Technical Adult School, Oakland, California.
    It focuses on the experience of Negroes in the program.

219. Evans, James C. "Adult Education Programs for Negroes in the Armed Forces." Journal of Negro Education, 45:437-442 (Summer, 1945).

A description of four educational programs, the Special Training Units, Professional and Technical Training, the Armed Forces Institute and Regular training programs, the article provides, at best, a general survey and fails to address the problem of discrimination, especially in the admission of blacks to the advanced programs.

220. Fisher, Paul L., and Ralph L. Lowenstein. Race and the News Media. New York: Frederick A. Praeger, Publisher, 1967.

The Negro newspaper is recognized as one of the most effective tools for educating the adult Negro population. The authors deal extensively with the Negro newspaper. Specifically, they address the "Newspaper Myths" and "The Role of the Negro Press in the Civil-Rights Struggle."

221. Freund, Eugene H., and Earl G. Stormo. "A Resocialization Strategy for Black Vietnam Veterans." Journal of Negro Education, 48:500-572 (Fall, 1979).

This article describes the Veterans in the Education (VIE) program at the University of Nebraska at Omaha. It is a program "which places underemployed or unemployed black males into productive positions in the labor force" and assists in upgrading their education skills.

222. Gandy, Samuel L. "The Negro Church and the Adult Education Phases of its Program." Journal of Negro Education, 14:381-384 (Summer, 1945).

Gandy provides a negative assessment of the black church's role in adult education. He cites four factors contributing to the church's limited role in adult education: an overt emphasis on paying church debts, ministerial training focusing primarily on saving souls and raising money, reliance on voluntary leadership which is sporadic and a religious attitude which is evangelical and anti social gospel in emphasis.

223. Gardiner, Betty, and Bettye Thomas. "The Cultural Impact of the Howard Theatre on the Black Community." Journal of Negro History, 55:253-265 (October, 1970).

The authors trace the evolution of Howard Theatre in Washington. D.C., from its inception in 1910 to its decline in 1960 and seek to ascertain its influence on the black community. In the first decades of its existence it served primarily the black middle class and was used not only for theatrical productions, vaudevilles and musicals but also for local variety programs, testimonials and church organizations. Once the Howard Theatre neighborhood began to deteriorate in the 1950's, the Theatre itself began to decline in importance, a further evidence of its middle-class clientele.

224. Ginzberg, Eli. The Negro Potential. New York: Columbia University Press, 1956.

The period addressed in this book is the 1950's.  The author
explores the potential of the American Negro as a gainfully employed,
socially adjusted and productive citizen.  He considers the lack of
basic education among Negro men and women as perhaps the most
inhibiting factor blocking the Negro race from reaching its fullest
potential.

225.  Godbey, Gordon C.  "The Negro and Adult Education:  Some References
from Selected Literature, 1942-1958."  Adult Leadership, 18:309 (April,
1970).

This article reviews four journals published by the Adult Education
Association of the U.S.A. during the years 1942-1948 to identify
articles, book reviews, programs, experiments or other forms of
adult education that focused on the American Negro.

226.  Gower, Calvin W.  "The Struggle of Blacks for Leadership Positions
in the Civilian Conservation Corps:  1933-1942."  Journal of Negro
History, 61:123-135 (April, 1976).

This article deals primarily with the blacks' struggle for leadership
positions in the Civilian Conservation Corps; however, the author
also alludes to the training blacks received in the Corps to enable
them to function effectively.

227.  Grant, Nancy L.  "Blacks, Regional Planning, and the TVA."  Ph.D.
dissertation, University of Chicago, 1978.  Pp. 201-260.

Chapter 6 of this dissertation is devoted to the hiring and
promotion practices of the Tennessee Valley Authority (TVA).  In
order for TVA to secure the quality personnel it needed for the
many available skilled positions, it provided numerous educational
and training opportunities for citizens of the valley.  A large
number of those who availed themselves of these opportunities were
black adults.

Between 1933 and 1943, TVA began construction on thirteen dams.
Workers were needed for three phases of construction.  The first
phase consisted of reservoir clearance work.  Men chopped trees,
cleared shrubbery, leveled the land and demolished or burned
condemned structures as well as constructed dirt roads.  The second
phase consisted of construction of the outer structure as well as
the base of the dam.  Workers skilled in carpentry, masonry and
cement finishing as well as operators of heavy construction
machinery were needed.  The third phase consisted of the installation
of the machinery to generate electricity and the mechanism to move
the locks that regulated the flow of the Tennessee River during
flood season.  Skilled technicians trained in mechanical and
electrical engineering were needed for this phase.

The author maintains that discriminatory practices against blacks
were widespread in TVA with regard to housing, hiring, promotion and
education and training.  Black employees were often replaced by
whites and terminated in groups.  They were denied entrance to
certain TVA sponsored apprenticeship programs.  With few exceptions
only "Negro" jobs and training programs  were open to them.

Training programs for "Negro trades" prepared blacks to be janitors, powdermen, jackhammer operators and wagon drill operators--the most menial and least desirable of all of TVA's apprenticeship programs.

228. _____. "Government Social Planning and Education for Blacks: The TVA Experiment 1933-1945." In Ronald K. Goodenow and Art White, eds. Education and the Rise of the New South. Boston: G. K. Hall, 1981. Pp. 215-236.

Grant provides an excellent analysis of the discriminatory practices within the TVA's experience in black adult education. She goes beyond the surface level of describing programs and citing of numbers to analyze the outcomes of the TVA programs for blacks, asking not only how many blacks were admitted but also what they received once they were admitted. Grant argues that TVA never reconciled the conflict between the agency's promise of non-discrimination with its respect for local customs and sensitivities to racial mores. In the end TVA officials, trade unions, politicians and local inhabitants all worked to block the implementation of effective programs in black education. TVA programs were both separated and unequal; relegating blacks into training programs for janitorial services, housework, agriculture and to those semi-skilled programs traditionally open to blacks. In the end, programs for whites were future-oriented while programs for blacks perpetuated the status quo.

229. Hall, Wiley A. "Adult Education Programs of Labor Unions and Other Workers' Groups." Journal of Negro Education, 14:407-411 (Summer, 1945).

Wiley highlights three types of educational programs of Labor Unions open to the blacks since the CIO was organized. These include educational programs conducted by the Union leadership, educational programs conducted for unions but by agencies outside the union and general programs with educational value. Basically descriptive in nature, the article does not make clear to what extent the programs cited are the exception rather than the norm for blacks.

230. Harrison, Bennett. Education Training and the Urban Ghetto. Baltimore, Md.: Johns Hopkins University Press, 1972.

This book provides a brief analysis of the "hard-core" unemployed's plight in America. Education is considered vital to their survival.

231. Height, Dorothy J. "The Adult Education Program of the YWCA Among Negroes." Journal of Negro Education, 14:390-395 (Summer, 1945).

Two contributions of the YWCA are noted. One is the YWCA Conferences which were racially intergrated and provided for many participants their first interracial experience. The other is the local YWCA's numerous projects, activities and programs including projects focusing on careers and art, trade schools, leadership training and clinics for black adult women entering jobs in industry or with governments.

232.   Heningburg, Alphonse.   "Adult Education and the National Urban
League."   Journal of Negro Education, 14:396-402 (Summer, 1945).

Included is a brief description of the National Urban League's adult
education programs in the following five areas:   industrial relations
laboratory, adult education in National Urban League cities, the
vocational opportunity campaigns, community relations project and
department of public relations or public education.   The League's
programs, based in part on a self-help philosophy, were designed for
both black and white adults.

233.   Hill, Herbert.   "Employment, Manpower Training and the Black
Worker."   Journal of Negro Education, 38:204-217 (Summer, 1969).

This article is an analysis of the impact the Federal Government
sponsored Manpower Development Training program had on the employment status of the black worker during 1968-1969.   The author
criticizes the disproportionate number of blacks receiving training
and employment through this program.

234.   Holley, Donald.   "The Negro in the New Deal Resettlement Program."
Agricultural History, 45:179-193 (July, 1971).

Holley argues that the Farm Security Administration and the
Resettlement Administration "left the best records in the New Deal
for providing equitable treatment for Negroes."   Although the main
thrust of the article does not deal with adult education, mention
is made of the hiring of black personnel to visit homes and farms in
order to assist in the family's planning of home and farm operations.

235.   Holmes, Eugene C.   "Alain L. Locke and the Adult Education
Movement."   Journal of Negro Education, 34:5-10 (Winter, 1965).

This article highlights the contributions of an eminent scholar and
eloquent spokesman for adult education, Alain L. Locke.   Educated at
Harvard, Oxford and the University of Berlin, Locke became a
prominent leader in the field of adult education.   He served as
president of the Adult Education Association of America from 1945-
1946, the first black to hold the position.

236.   Horne, Frank S., and Corienne K. Robinson.   "Adult Educational
Programs in Housing Projects with Negro Tenants."   Journal of Negro
Education, 14:353-362 (Summer, 1945).

In September, 1944, an estimated 410,000 blacks lived in public
housing projects including 90,000 adults living in slum-clearance,
low-rent housing developments.   The article describes community-
sponsored adult educational activities and programs available to the
tenants.   Some activities were racially intergrated, some partially
intergrated, while others were totally segregated.

237.   House, Secil V.   "The Implications of Dr. Martin Luther King, Jr's
Work and Philosophy for the Field of Adult Education."   Ph.D.
dissertation, Indiana University, 1975.

House points out that Dr. Martin Luther King was indeed an adult educator. His influence as a black teacher in America was perhaps as pronounced as any in the history of this country. This study examines the philosophy and work of Dr. King relative to their implications for adult education.

238. _____. "Implications of Martin Luther King, Jr.'s Work and Philosophy for Adult Education." Adult Leadership, 25:229 (April, 1977).

The author contends that Martin Luther King was an adult educator. Manifestations of his concern for the education of black adults were exemplified in his work and the philosophy he espoused.

239. Hubert, Giles A. "Some Recent Developments in Adult Education Among Negroes in Agriculture." Journal of Negro Education, 14:341-346 (Summer, 1945).

Hubert provides a brief survey of New Deal Programs, many informal in nature, designed to bolster the sagging agricultural economy and provide training for black farmers. These included organizing neighborhood and community discussion groups to provide aid in farm planning and training in record keeping. The latter was especially noteworthy since record keeping by black tenants had formerly been viewed by some as a sign of rebelliousness on the part of the tenant.

240. Jackson, Luther P. "Citizenship Training--A Neglected Area in Adult Education." Journal of Negro Education, 14:477-487 (Summer, 1945).

Jackson explores the need for and describes selected efforts in citizenship training for black adults. Most noteworthy are descriptions of the Virginia Voter League's and Virginia State Teachers Association's efforts in preparing blacks to qualify for and instructing them in the use of the ballot.

241. Johnson, Campbell C. "The Negro Youth and the Educational Program of the Y.M.C.A." Journal of Negro Education, 9:354-362 (July, 1940).

Johnson traces the early history of the YMCA and describes its changing emphasis in program offerings from a focus an evangel-ization prior to 1912 to a more diverse educational program indluding recreation, employment bureaus, adult educational programs, lectures and social activities. Surprisingly, the adult education programs, described by Campbell, were predominantly sponsored by those local YMCAs which were not housed in buildings specifically constructed as YMCA centers.

242. Johnson, Earl S. "The Need for a Philosophy of Adult Education." Journal of Negro Education, 14:272-282 (Summer, 1945).

Johnson criticizes the narrow vocational emphasis in adult education programs.

243. Kahlenberg, Richard S. "Negro Radio." Negro History Bulletin, 29:127-128, 142-143 (March, 1966).

The article provides a brief discussion of Negro radio, including
its early history and the importance of Negro radio in promoting
black identity.

244.  Kling, Martin, and Bonnie Tivenan.  "Reading Activities of Black
Adult Students."  Adult Education, 28:156-164 (Spring, 1978).

This study describes the reading activities of adult black high
school equivalency students.

245.  Lane, David A.  "An Army Project in the Duty-Time General
Education of Negro Troops in Europe, 1947-1951."  Journal of Negro
Education, 33:117-124 (Spring, 1964).

This is a report on a project to upgrade the literacy skills of
U.S. Army Negro troops in Europe who scored low on the Army General
Classification Test.

246.  Lane, Frayzer T.  "Section H:  An Educational Program for the
Adjustment of Negroes to Urban Living."  Journal of Negro Education,
14:117-122 (Winter, 1945).

Lane briefly describes the Chicago Urban League's attempt to help
in-migrants from the South adjust to urban living.  The conservative
nature of the program is evident, with its emphasis on self-reliance,
cleanliness and industriousness.

247.  Lawson, Marjorie McKenzie.  "The Adult Education Aspects of the
Negro Press."  Journal of Negro Education, 14:431-436 (Summer, 1945).

Lawson reports on the findings of a survey of forty-nine editors of
black magazines which solicited their views on the appropriate role
of the black newspaper in educating the black reader and inculcating
race pride.

248.  Lawson, Steven F.  Black Ballots:  Voting Rights in the South,
1944-1969.  New York:  Columbia University Press, 1976.

This book is a study of the process by which black adults in the
South gained the right to vote.  It shows how the legal and
political institutions of the United States responded to the demands
by blacks to have the Fifteenth Amendment enforced.  The civil
rights organizations that took the lead in protesting the denial of
black voting rights were the NAACP and the Student Non Violent
Coordinating Committee (SNCC).  The many years of protest against
black disenfranchisement resulted in the enactment and implementation
of a Voting Rights Act.  The voting right experience alone was
educational for black adults.

249.  Lenroot, Karen F.  "The Children's Bureau and Health Education."
Journal of Negro Education, 18:388-397 (Summer, 1949).

Lenroot surveys the role of the "Children's Bureau" in providing
both health services and health education.  Of special interest is
her discussion of the Herman G. Morgan Health Center's activities in

Indianapolis, including its work with Flanner House, a social settlement center open to both black and white in-migrants from the South.

250. Levitan, Sar A., et al.  Still a Dream.  Cambridge, Mass.: Harvard University Press, 1975.

The author discusses the pros and cons of Federally initiated man-power training for the disadvantaged.  The primary purpose of the program was to improve the economic and social conditions of the disadvantaged.

251. Lloyd, Gil B.  "A Quarter Century of the Black Experience with the Church, 1950-1974."  The Negro Educational Review, 27:34-44 (Jan., 1976).

Lloyd presents a highly laudatory account of the black church's role in improving a quality of life he calls "'first-classness' meaning first-class personhood, first-class citizenship, first-class opportunity, and first-class responsibility."

252. Locke, Alain L.  "Areas of Extension and Improvement of Adult Education Among Negroes."  Journal of Negro Education, 14:453-459 (Summer, 1945).

Locke provides a critical assessment of adult education programs for blacks.  He criticizes adult education programs which include anything and everything in non-planned informal activities and calls for a removal of vague and amateurish programs.  Secondly, he applauds the trend toward  integration and warns that the more "chauvinistic" Negro organizations will face increasing competition as society becomes more integrated.

253. _____.  "The Intellectual Interests of Negroes."  Journal of Adult Education, 8:352 (June, 1936).

The article contains Locke's philosophy of black education.  He maintains that the issue of "race" should be the focal point for mass adult education, arguing that activities centered around racial issues would create much interest among Negro adults.

254. Mangum, Garth L.  MDTA:  Foundation of Federal Manpower Policy. Baltimore:  Johns Hopkins Press, 1968.

The Man Power Development Training Act (MDTA) "was passed primarily on the assumption that widespread job vacancies existed and that unemployment could be reduced by training the unemployed to fill them."  Thousands of blacks received training under this program. This book is part of a continuing evaluation of the Federal manpower policies and programs.

255. Marshall, Ray.  The Negro Worker.  New York:  Random House, 1967.

Marshall includes a brief section on the education of and apprenticeship training for blacks.  He underscores the importance of the apprenticeship programs noting that vocational training has rarely supplied sufficient practical and theoretical training necessary for a skilled craftsman. He concludes that the Manpower Development and Training (MDTA), Area Redevelopment (ARA) and Economic Opportunity (EOA) programs were moderately successful especially in their enrollment of blacks in clerical, sales, skilled and semi-skilled categories. Despite their success, however, non-whites were not being upgraded in the job sector comparably to whites, nor were they having equal access to on-the-job training programs and job placement.

256. _____, and Vernon M. Briggs. Equal Apprenticeship Opportunities. Ann Arbor: University of Michigan, Institute of Labor and Industrial Relations, 1968.

One of the critical problems in the apprenticeship system is the paucity of black enrollees. Many of America's most skilled journeymen received their training through apprenticeship programs. Apprenticeship programs are generally among the best adult education programs available. This monograph discusses the nature of apprenticeship and describes a successful and well-integrated program in New York City.

257. _____. The Negro and Apprenticeship. Baltimore: The Johns Hopkins Press, 1967.

Although published in 1967, this book is still one of the most comprehensive resources on the subject of Negro Apprenticeship in the United States. It provides a general overview of apprenticeship training as well as details regarding Negro participation in the apprenticeship enterprise. It also focuses on the discriminatory practices employed by union officials in different cities to exclude Negroes from the various apprenticeship programs.

258. _____. "Negro Participation in Apprenticeship Programs." Journal of Human Resources, 15:51-69 (Winter, 1967).

This article is the result of a study of Negro participation in selected apprenticeship programs. It concludes that discrimination is the major factor inhibiting Negro participation. Recommendations are also made to deal with the paucity of Negro representation.

259. Mathews, Donald R., and James W. Prothro. Negroes and the New Southern Politics. New York: Harcourt-Brace, 1966.

One of the most effective tools in the political arena for educating the black adult masses is the black church. The author describes this tool in a chapter entitled "The Negro Church and Politics."

260. Mays, B. E. "The Education of Negro Ministers." Journal of Negro Education, 2:342-351 (July, 1933).

Mays describes the educational status of and efforts in self-improvement by black ministers.

261. McAlister, Jane E., and Dorothy M. McAllister. "Adult Education for Negroes in Rural Areas: The Work of the Jeanes Teachers and Home Farm Demonstration Agents." Journal of Negro Education, 14:331-340 (Summer, 1945).

Based on information gained from reports of Home and Farm Agents and from returned questionnaires of Jeanes supervisors, the authors reach the following conclusions: although Home and Farm Agents and Jeanes supervisors provide aid in coordinating community education efforts in the areas of health, making a living, recreation and home-making, the effects of their work is often temporary; the Home and Farm Agents focus primarily on simple how-to-do activities, and the Jeanes teachers have only recently grasped the importance of the school in community education.

262. McGee, Leo. "Black Rural Land Decline in the South." The Black Scholar, 8:8-11 (May, 1977).

Lack of adequate formal education is cited as one of the major reasons for the precipitous decline of black landownership. This article highlights the sociological, economical and political implications of black land decline and stresses the need for blacks to become more knowledgeable in the real estate field.

263. Medoff, Marshall H. "Discrimination: Blacks and the Apprentice-ship Trade Programs." The Negro Educational Review, 26:147-154 (October, 1975).

Medoff provides an excellent critical analysis of the discriminatory practices in apprenticeship trade programs. He examines and rejects two arguments that have been used to explain why only 4.6 percent of apprenticeship trade program enrollees were black, namely that blacks have a higher discount rate in future earnings than whites and that blacks have a shorter life expectancy and higher illness rate. He concludes that the major reason for low minority participation in the programs is the discriminatory practices of trade unions which possess near monopoly power.

264. Menchan, W. McKinley. "Adult Education Programs of Negro Parent-Teacher Associations." Journal of Negro Education, 14:412-417 (Summer, 1945).

The article describes Negro Parent-Teacher Associations' involvement in adult education based on information supplied by eleven state presidents. Activities include leadership training for PTA leaders, home study educational programs, remedial education and occupational training and cultural improvement. A common problem cited is the lack of interest on the part of the parents and/or school principals.

265. Mirengoff, William. The Comprehensive Employment Training Act: An Interim Report. Washington, D.C.: National Academy of Sciences, 1976.

This book is an interim report/evaluation of the Comprehensive Employment Training Act. The main emphasis of the Program was job training for the unemployed from the disadvantaged stratum of the American society. Many black adults participated in this program.

266. _____, and Lester Rindler. CETA: Manpower Programs Under Local Control. Washington, D.C.: National Academy of Sciences, 1978.

This is a comprehensive report of the Comprehensive Employment
Training Act.

267.  Mitchell, Eva C.  "Adult Health Education and Recreational
Programs:  National, State, and Local."  Journal of Negro Education,
14:363-373 (Summer, 1945).

Mitchell surveyed existing health program activities and agencies in
five areas including national agencies, selected states' adult health
education programs, local health education programs, recreational
activities and health education literature for laymen.  She concludes
that health and recreational problems were most severe in those
areas where the black population equaled or exceeded the white
population and that rural blacks had least access to health clinics.

268.  Morton, Mary A.  "The Education of Negroes in the District of
Columbia."  Journal of Negro Education, 16:325-339 (Summer, 1947).

Included in the description of educational development in the
nation's capital from 1930-1947 is a brief discussion on the
expansion of evening schools and educational activities for veterans.

269.  Mueller, Ruth Caston.  "The National Council of Negro Women, Inc."
Negro History Bulletin, 18:27-31 (November, 1954).

Mueller notes the educational activities of the National Council of
Negro Women including the education of Negro women in citizenship
rights and responsibilities, world affairs and training of women in
leadership skills.

270.  Oxley, Howard W.  "The Civilian Conservation Corps and the
Education of the Negro."  Journal of Negro Education, 7:375-382 (July,
1938).

Oxley's article presents the "public" posture of the CCC.
Publically it proclaimed as its "policy in CCC education to seek to
motivate and develop every enrollee, regardless of race or creed, to
his fullest capacity."  In seeking to demonstrate that this policy
was implemented, Oxley describes the varied educational programs
available to blacks, especially in literacy training, elementary-
level schooling and vocational programs to enhance the black
youth's employability.  No mention is made of the CCC's
discriminatory policy in the enrollment of blacks.  Nor is an
attempt made to analyze whether or not blacks were disproportionately
placed in vocational courses emphasizing those skills preparing the
blacks for jobs traditionally open to them.

271.  Parsons, Talcott, and Kenneth B. Clark.  The Negro American.
Boston:  Houghton Mifflin, 1966.

Lyndon B. Johnson sets the tone for this publication.  In the
Foreword he declares that "Nothing is of greater significance to
the welfare and vitality of this nation than the movement to secure
equal rights for Negro Americans."  This book is a collection of
essays dealing with many subjects relating to the Negro's struggle

for equality. In the essay entitled "Demographic Factors in the Integration of the Negro," the author admonishes that:

". . . the Negro adult must not be ignored, especially the Negro adult male, who may be beyond the age at which it is possible to acquire skills which permit him to make his own way . . . serious consideration should be given to the development of intensive labor projects on which such adult Negroes can be usefully employed. . . . It is highly probable that programs of the type suggested would, in the long run, be less expensive than the present combination of inadequate educational training facilities and wasted human resources resulting from unemployment, welfare and relief, delinquency and crime, and high morbidity and mortality."

272. Partridge, Deborah Canon. "Adult Education Projects Sponsored by Negro College Fraternities and Sororities." Journal of Negro Education, 14:374–380 (Summer, 1945).

An expanded notion of service led sororities and fraternities to become involved in adult education. This article, based on responses to a questionnaire sent to sixty-four black colleges and to the fraternities' and sororities' national offices, provides a brief description of the projects sponsored by the Greek letter organizations. Conclusions reached in the study included: most significant programs were sponsored by graduate chapters; most were aimed at an urban population; only a small percentage of Greek letter organizations sponsored educational programs; and, the most common programs were aimed at increased participation in civil life or were focused on vocational education.

273. Patten, Thomas II. Manpower Planning and the Development of Human Resources. New York: Wiley-Interscience, 1971.

The main focus of this book regarding black adult education is the apprenticeship system. The author points to the many glaring discriminatory practices associated with the system, thereby preventing blacks from fully benefiting from this training program.

274. Pettigrew, Thomas F. A Profile of the Negro American. Princeton, N.J.: D. Van Nostrand Co., Inc., 1964.

Included in this "Profile of the Negro American," is a brief discussion on the educational gains of the Negro adult population from 1940 to 1960.

275. Phipard, Ester F. "The Participation of Government Agencies in a Nutrition Program." Journal of Negro Education, 18:390–408 (Summer, 1949).

The author describes the educational activities in farm-and-home guidance and nutrition education by the USDA, Farmers Home Administration, Federal Security Agency and American National Red Cross Nutrition Service. Written in the Booker T. Washington tradition of self-help, the article ignores the history of racial discrimination in these agencies.

276.  Redd, George N.  "Adult Education for Negroes Under Public School
Auspices."  Journal of Negro Education, 14:312-321 (Summer, 1945).

Redd analyzed the administration of, participation in and types of
programs available for blacks under public school auspices in state
and city adult education programs.  Some of his conclusions are:
except for Federally funded programs there has been little evidence
of state activity in adult programs, urban public school systems
have not met urban needs; the primary emphasis to date has been on
literacy and low-level skills training programs; and, in most
instances the quantity and quality of black programs have not been
equal to those for whites, and the best programs are in those border
cities which have large centers of black population.

277.  Reddick, L. D.  "Adult Education and the Improvement of Race
Relations."  Journal of Negro Education, 14:488-493 (Summer, 1945).

Reddick makes a stinging critique of adult education programs, a
critique that was conspicuously absent in most discussions of black
adult education both in the Journal of Negro Education and the
Journal of Negro History prior to the mid-twentieth century.  He
criticizes both the black and the white spokesmen at black
conferences who failed to adequately deal with the race problem and
only counseled patience.  He argues that adult education has failed
to embrace the improvement of race relations as part of its program
for several reasons including the red tape and terror imposed on
personnel by Federal programs, the American Association for Adult
Education's emphasis on the "strictly 'cultural' side of adult
education" and the traditional American emphasis upon individualism.
Although written in 1945 it still remains an excellent critique of
the bland, social advoidance stance evident in much of the official
adult education programs and publications.

278.  _____.  "The Negro in the United States Navy During World
War II."  Journal of Negro History, 32:201-219 (January, 1947).

Reddick traces the discriminatory and exclusionist policies of the
U.S. Navy from 1920 to World War II.  By the summer of 1942,
manpower needs forced the administration to move beyond training
blacks only as messmen and placing them in segregated facilities.
This made possible the entry of blacks into a variety of skills-
training programs.  Although the focus of the paper is in the Navy's
changing policy regarding the black servicemen it also provides a
description of numerous trades open to blacks after 1942.

279.  Reedy, Sidney J.  "The Negro Magazine:  A Critical Study of Its
Educational Significance."  Journal of Negro Education, 3:598-604
(October, 1934).

Reedy analyzes the role of five leading black magazines and
periodicals--Opportunity, The Crisis, The Messenger, The Southern
Workman and the Journal of Negro History--in educating the black
community.  Topics emphasized most in these magazines were
vocational, leisure-time and citizenship education.  Topics
mentioned less frequently were ethical character, health, command of

fundamental processes and worthy home membership. Lacking was
material explaining how some of these goals or topics might be
achieved.

280.  Reid, Ira De A.  "The Development of Adult Education for Negroes
in the United States."  Journal of Negro Education, 14:299–306 (Summer,
1945).

Reid provides a brief survey of the rise and development of adult
education programs for blacks from the Colonial era to the New Deal.
The article highlights the importance of the abolitionists, the
Civil War, the churches, Hampton and Tuskegee and, above all, the
New Deal Agencies and Foundations in promoting educational programs
and activities.  Unlike many other writers on black adult education
prior to 1945, Reid recognizes the impact of the race issue on the
development of adult educational programs for blacks.

281.  Resnick, Solmon, and Barbara Kaplan.  "College Programs for Black
Adults."  Journal of Higher Education, 42:202–218 (March, 1971).

The authors explain the need for and describe their experience with
two programs designed specifically for black adults.  The Queens
College Adult Continuing Education Program (1965) accepted a group
of Puerto Ricans and blacks despite low test scores and emphasized
development of academic skills.  The Seek Program (1966) broke with
the traditional course content and utilized two new courses, English
and Social Science, to teach "college skills."

282.  Roberts, Harry W.  "The Rural Negro Minister:  His Educational
Status."  Journal of Negro Education, 17:478–487 (Fall, 1948).

This description of the educational status of and efforts in
continuing education by rural ministers was based on a survey of
clergy attending summer schools for ministers at Virginia State
College from 1943–1946.  The most significant finding was that rural
ministers with high school or college education were more likely to
participate in continuing educational programs than were their less
educated counterparts.  Given the fact that 31 percent of the rural
pastors surveyed had a eighth grade education or less, the findings
left little hope that adult or continuing education was having a
significant impact upon that group of rural ministers who needed it
the most.

283.  Roberts, S. O.  "The Education of Negroes in Tennessee."  Journal
of Negro Education, 16:417–424 (Summer, 1947).

The importance of Roberts' brief discussion on vocational education
for blacks in the mid-1940's is that it clearly demonstrates the
lingering effects of racism in occupational training.

284.  Rose, Arnold.  Assuring Freedom to the Free.  Detroit:  Wayne
State University Press, 1964.

Rose addresses two topics which have relevance for the study of the
education of the black adult, the church and the skilled trades.
He contends that the church is the major social institution within

the black community and historically has played an important role in
education. Rose highlights the inequity in the skill trades and
apprenticeship programs when comparing black and white participation.
Yet the apprenticeship programs have offered excellent educational
opportunities for young adults.

285. Rose, Ernestine. "The Harlem Experiment." Journal of Adult
Education, 8:352-353 (June, 1936).

This article describes one of the most noted and successful Negro
adult education projects in American history, the "Harlem Experiment." This was a library-centered project which experimented with
numerous educational activities for the Negro adult in Harlem.

286. Salmond, John A. "The Civilian Conservation Corps and the Negro."
Journal of American History, 52:75-88 (January, 1965).

Salmond's definitive essay on the CCC's policy relative to the black
males goes beyond Howard Oxley's laudatory, surface-level
descriptions to analyzing the Corps'"official policy which prevented
full participation by Negroes." The Corps' policy of establishing
segregated camps, of assigning enrollees to camps in their home
state, the attitudes of local selection agents in the South and
especially of the CCC's director, Robert Fechner, and a lack of a
concerted effort on the part of President F. D. Roosevelt, himself,
all contributed toward limiting the participation of blacks.
Salmond does note the Corps' contributions, including educational
training in academic and vocational areas, for blacks who were
enrolled. The failure of the CCC was "not one of performance"
measured by what it did for those who enrolled, but rather "one of
potential," what it could have done if more had been enrolled.

287. Stokes, Olivia P. "Education in the Black Church: Design for
Change." Religious Education, 64:433-455 (July-August, 1974).

The author argues that it is essential that the black church behave
as a viable educational unit within the black community. Rationale
for this contention as well as suggested educational programs are
provided.

288. Thompson, Charles H. "The Federal Program of Vocational Education
in Negro Schools of Less than College Grade." Journal of Negro
Education, 76:303-318 (July, 1938).

Thompson describes the programs and administration and legislation
governing Federal programs of vocational education in schools of
less than college grade in the seventeen states having legally
segregated systems. Blacks were underrepresented in all programs,
especially in trades and industry programs. He concludes that there
seems to be a "deliberate policy to provide Negroes with as little
trade training as possible."

289. "Training Louisiana Leaders." Negro History Bulletin, 18:7-8
(October, 1954).

The article includes a description of a one-week training program in the 3 R's of politics, government and education for leaders and potential leaders sponsored by the Masons and the Louisiana Education Association.

290.  Webster, Sherman N.  "A Study of the Patterns of Adult Education in Selected Negro Churches."  Ed.D dissertation, Indiana University, 1959.

Throughout the history of America, the church has been one of the strongest educational resources for the Negro adult, especially in the realm of moral and intellectual stimulation of the masses.  The purpose of this study was to ascertain the patterns of adult education in ten Baptist Negro churches, each located in a different city.  The study focuses specifically on the adult leaders, the participants, educational programming, instructional methods, subjects taught, program goals and evaluation.

291.  Wilkerson, Doxey A.  "The Negro Press."  Journal of Negro Education, 16:511-521 (Fall, 1947).

Wilkerson discusses the content and emphasis of the Negro press and its availability to the black community.  He emphasizes its role as interpreter of current developments for the black community.

292.  _____.  "The Participation of Negroes in the Federally-Aided Program of Agricultural and Home Economics Extension."  Journal of Negro Education 7:331-344 (July, 1938).

Wilkerson analyzes the extent to which blacks participated in Federally aided programs of agricultural and home economics extension in sixteen Southern states having dejure segregation and containing 96 percent of the country's rural black population.  He notes that whereas blacks constituted 24.2 percent of the rural population they received only 6.2 percent of the Federal funds spent on cooperative extension work and concludes that disparity in expenditures was directly linked to a "system of caste which defines for Negro Americans a position on the very margins of our country."

An excellent study, it is one of the few articles published prior to World War II which dealt with the impact of racism in adult educational programs.

293.  _____.  "Section E:  The Vocational Education and Guidance of Negroes:  The Negro and the Battle of Production."  Journal of Negro Education, 11:228-239 (April, 1942).

The author reports on a survey which showed the continuing wide-spread discrimination in war-production employment but also the beginning of a trend to relaxation of social barriers in hiring due to war production demands.  The immediate problem facing blacks was the need for pre-employment training programs, refresher courses for blacks on the job to open up opportunities for advancement and out-of-school youth defense training programs, especially for rural youth ages 18-25.  Nearly two-thirds of blacks enrolled in pre-employment and supplementary training programs were in automotive

services, machine shop, welding, aviation services, sheet-metal
work, electrical services and foundry, areas not necessarily
associated with traditional jobs for blacks. In the agricultural
sector, however, much of the money for the support of the extension
agents went to the service of the white farmers.

294. _____. Special Problems of Negro Education. Washington,
D.C.: Government Printing Office, 1939. Pp. 135-136.

In 1933 the Federal Emergency Relief Administration initiated a
number of educational programs for adults. The most extensive of
these were literary education, general adult education and vocational
training. In 1935 a comprehensive survey was undertaken of the
adult education activities in the South. This book contains a brief
report of the findings of the study which covered adult education
enrollments, teachers and salaries in programs sponsored by the
Federal Government in thirteen Southern states.

295. _____, and Lemuel A. Penn. "The Participation of Negroes
in the Federally-Aided Program of Civilian Vocational Rehabilitation."
Journal of Negro Education, 7:319-330 (July, 1938).

The authors analyze the degree of black participation in Federally
aided programs for physically handicapped, civilian adults.
Specifically, they focus on: (1) the purpose of vocational
rehabilitation, (2) the extent of black participation, (3) legislative and administrative conditions which influenced black
participation and (4) modifications necessary to protect black
interests. Noteable findings included: (1) in sixteen Southern
states blacks constituted 24.4 percent of the total populations but
only 8.2 percent of the cases closed by vocational rehabilitation,
(2) 55.7 percent of black but only 24.8 percent of white rehabilitants
received services which did not include vocational training and (3)
three times as many blacks as whites received services which were
limited to the receipt of artificial appliances. The authors
concluded: "Whereas the major services rendered to white clients is
vocational training, the chief services rendered to Negro clients
is prosthesis."

296. Wilkins, Roy. "Adult Education Programs of the NAACP." Journal
of Negro Education, 14:403-406 (Summer, 1945).

Wilkins briefly describes the following adult education programs and
activities: sponsoring leadership training conferences, motivating
local groups to study their state and/or local education, stimulating
groups to study the political system, educating white society on
race issues and encouraging groups to study restrictions in employment and housing.

297. Williams, Dorothy G. "Adult Education in Public Libraries and
Museums." Journal of Negro Education, 14:322-330 (Summer, 1945).

The author describes the types of adult educational activities
undertaken by public libraries and museums and notes their
concentration in Northern urban centers.

298.  Williams, Lillian S.  "To Elevate the Race:  The Michigan Avenue
YMCA and the Advancement of Blacks in Buffalo, New York, 1922-1940."
In Vincent P. Franklin and James D. Anderson, eds.  New Perspectives
on Black Educational History.  Boston:  G. K. Hall, 1978.  Pp. 129-148.

   William's essay describes and analyzes the establishment and
   contribution of a Buffalo YMCA during a period of rapid in-migration
   of blacks, increased discrimination and racial segregation.  The
   author describes the YMCA's far ranging programs for boys, young
   adults and for the black community in general.  Included in its
   programs were physical education, occupational training, music,
   public forums, lectures and health education.  Williams concludes
   that despite the seemingly conservative stance of the black YMCA
   officials, the Michigan Avenue YMCA did serve as a "force in
   elevating or improving the social, cultural, intellectual, and
   educational conditions of that community."  Unlike some of the early
   articles dealing with the YMCA in the black community, William's
   essay moves beyond a simple description of programs to an analysis
   of the role of the YMCA in a racist society.

299.  Wolfe, Joseph A.  "Increasing Black Entrepreneurship in the Ghetto:
An Exploratory Study of A Management Training Program for Harlem Blacks."
Ph.D dissertation, New York University, 1971.

   This study examines the Workshop in Business Opportunities, a
   management training program in the Harlem community in New York City
   designed to increase black entrepreneurship in the city.  The author
   also presents an extensive list of conclusions.

300.  Wolters, Raymond.  Negroes and the Great Depression.  Westport,
Conn.:  Greenwood Publishing Corp., 1938.

   Included in this book is a discussion on the Works Progress
   Administration during the Great Depression which proved to be a
   benefit to thousands of blacks.  The primary purpose of this Federal
   project was to provide employment and other assistance to the
   disadvantaged.  Much of this organization's activity was of an
   educational nature.  The author devotes a section of the book to
   this project.

301.  Woodson, Grace I.  "Community Related Programs at West Virginia
State College."  Journal of Negro Education, 16:594-596 (Fall, 1947).

   The author provides a brief description of community related
   programs in various disciplines including the Department of
   Economics, Department of Business Administration, Department of
   Health, Physical Education and Safety Education, Sociology and the
   Division of Mining--all demonstrating the College's philosophy that
   the community is the campus.

302.  Wormley, Margaret Just.  "Adult Education in Federal Prisons."
Journal of Negro Education, 45:425-430 (Summer, 1945).

   The author focuses on adult education programs in Federal prisons
   generally, taking at face value the statement of the Supervisor of
   Education in the U.S. Bureau of Prisons that all adult education

programs were non-segregated and hence all education programs were open to blacks. These programs included education of illiterates and near illiterates, practical trade training, specialized subjects, correspondence courses and health education. No data is included on the actual enrollment of black prisoners. It is not clear whether the article is more prescriptive than descriptive in nature.

303. Wright, Marion Thompson. "Negro Youth and the Federal Emergency Programs: CCC and NYA." Journal of Negro Education, 9:397-407 (July, 1940).

The author describes the educational activities provided by the CCC and NYA, discusses some of the problems facing these programs including the underrepresentation of blacks in the CCC and cites the need for the Federal Government to take a lead in opening up job opportunities for blacks.

304. Wright, Nathan. Black Power and Urban Unrest. New York: Hawthorn Books, Inc., 1967.

"Adult Priority Needs" is the title of a topic discussed in this book. The author is challenging the nation, from the Federal Government downward, to establish educational programs for black adults in urban areas. He calls for a bold legislative gesture, comparable to the one which created the Morrill Act to "do for Negroes in cities what the Morrill Act did for rural communities of the land."

305. _____. Let's Work Together. New York: Hawthorn Books, Inc., 1968.

Wright advocates job training programs for Negro adults. To some degree this approach can compensate for the inadequacies of the educational systems.

306. Wye, Christopher G. "The New Deal and the Negro Community: Toward a Broader Conceptualization." Journal of American History, 59:621-639 (December, 1972).

Using Cleveland as a case study, the author analyzes not only whether or not the blacks received their "proportionate share" from the New Deal programs but also the impact of these programs upon the autonomy of the Negro Community. He points out that although blacks received "more than their share" of jobs provided by the New Deal programs including the CCC and WPA they were disproportionately placed in low skill level jobs.

307. Young, Whitney M. To Be Equal. New York: McGraw-Hill Book Co., 1964.

The author is critical of the Manpower Development Training Act programs developed by the Federal Government in the 1960's for disadvantaged adults, because they were "out of touch with reality."

# 5
# GENERAL RESOURCES

308.  Adler, Mortimer, et al.  The Negro in American History.  New York:
Encyclopedia Britannica, 1953.

   Included among the extensive array of essays are several which deal
   with the education of the black adult.

309.  Aptheker, Herbert.  A Documentary History of the Negro People in
the United States.  New York:  The Citadel Press, 1965.

   Numerous aspects of Negro life are covered in this comprehensive
   history of the Afro-American.  Aptheker  mentions many organizations
   that contributed to black education including the churches, the
   Negro Educational Society and local, state and national conventions
   that contributed to and the importance of printed materials in black
   education.

310.  _____.  Essays in the History of the American Negro.  New
York:  International Publishers, 1945.

   Negroes participated in various capacities in both the American
   Revolution and the Civil War.  Both of these Wars contributed to
   their education; their participation alone was an education.

   This book discusses the blacks' contributions in the American
   Revolution and Civil War.

311.  _____.  To be Free:  Studies in American Negro History.
New York:  International Publishers, 1948.

   The Negro struggle for enfranchisement in America was educational in
   and of itself.  Strategizing, to accomplish this end, consistently
   tested the intellectual and physical abilities of Negroes
   individually and collectively.  This book details many significant
   historical episodes relative to Negro efforts for freedom and
   citizenship.

312. Baker, Robert A. The American Baptist Home Mission Society and the South, 1832-1894. Ph.D. dissertation, Yale University, 1947.

This dissertation provides a historical perspective on the American Baptist Home Mission Society and its activities in the South. It gives a brief account of the Society's emphasis on the education of black adults. Of special importance is the Society's efforts to train black ministers.

313. Banks, William L. The Black Church in the U.S. Chicago: Moody Press, 1972.

One of the most potent informal as well as formal educational institutions of the adult Negro masses is the Negro church. The author thoroughly analyzes the Negro church, its origin, contribution and outlook.

314. Bennett, Lerone. Before the Mayflower: A History of the Negro in America, 1614-1962. Chicago: Johnson Publishing Company, 1962.

Bennett points out that there were varying degrees of educational opportunities, both formal and informal, available to the black adult throughout their history. Numerous whites were sympathetic to and took risks in support of Negro education.

Even more significant were the efforts made by blacks themselves to improve every aspect of their lives, with education receiving top priority. This book cites four major avenues by which blacks attempted to expand their horizon educationally: (1) The Negro convention, headed by Frederick Douglass; (2) Negro church, initiation of a separate church for Negroes (African Methodist Episcopal Church) by Richard Allen and Absalom Jones; (3) Written Media, initiated by journalists such as Samuel Cornish and John Russwurm; and, (4) Negro Masonic Lodge, conceived by Prince Hall.

315. Bergman, Peter M. The Chronological History of the Negro in America. New York: Harper & Row, 1969.

In this chronological history of the Negro in America there are several indications that efforts were made to provide educational opportunities for the Negro adult. The chief sponsors of these were the Federal Government, through the Freedmen's Bureau and the Union Army, and religious and benevolent organizations.

316. Billingsley, Andrew. Black Families in White America. Englewood Cliffs, N.J.: Prentice-Hall, Inc., 1968.

This publication includes one section dealing with Negro adult education. Its assessment of the education of the black adult was not positive; only one-half of all Negro adults had completed at least one year of high school. Moreover, future predictions were also not positive.

317. Bracey, John H., et al. Black Nationalism in America. New York: Bobbs-Merrill, 1970.

Black nationalism in and of itself embodies educational overtones. It embraces social thought, attitudes and action ranging from the simplest expression of ethnocentrism to the severest forms of racial revolt.

Since the arrival of Africans on American soil, nationalist sentiment in various forms has been prominent in Negro thought. Various ideologies were expressed to combat racial injustices and to improve the educational, economic and social conditions of the nation's most oppressed people. The author explores black nationalist ideologies evident in the activities of religious denominations, civil rights organizations, the convention movement and in printed media and black oratories.

318. Brown, Ira C. Race Relations in a Democracy. New York: Harper and Row, 1949.

In the chapter entitled "Education and the Struggle for Advancement," the author alludes to the efforts of benevolent organizations and the Federal Government in providing education for the adult Negro.

319. Bullock, Henry A. A History of Negro Education in the South. Cambridge: Harvard University Press, 1967.

This is one of the standard histories of black education in the South. Although claiming to be a history of black education from 1619-1967, only one chapter is devoted to black education prior to the Civil War. While Bullock focuses primarily on formal education in the elementary and secondary schools and colleges, he does make mention of educational programs for black adults sponsored by organizations and benevolent societies including the Freedmen's Bureau and the Union Army.

320. Bullock, Penelope L. "The Negro Periodical Press in the United States, 1838-1909." Ph.D. dissertation, University of Michigan, 1971.

A history of black education in America is incomplete without including the contributions of the Negro press. Publication for mass distribution has been one of the most effective means of educating the masses. This dissertation identifies and describes Negro periodicals that were in circulation from 1838-1906.

321. Cain, Afred E. Negro Heritage Library. Chicago: Educational Heritage, Inc., 1965.

An extensive list of topics on Negro heritage is included in this voluminous publication. Those topics that are addressed which relate to the education of the Negro adult population include: (1) Negro newspapers, (2) Negro Conventions and (3) the Freedmen's Bureau.

322. Cartwright, Morse A. "The History of Adult Education in the United States." Journal of Negro Education, 14:283-292 (Summer, 1945).

Cartwright provides a sketchy history of adult education in America from the Colonial era to the twentieth century with special emphasis

on the education of the black adult.  Prior to the depression of the
1930's and the WPA, there was little provision made for black adult
education except for literacy training.  The WPA and the depression
changed the overt emphasis on assimilation prevalent in adult
education during World War I and the 1920's.  Mention is made of
agricultural extension, adult vocational education, worker's
education beginning with the International Ladies' Garment Workers'
Union, special schools, councils and formal organizations active in
promoting adult education.

323.  Collier-Thomas, Betty.  "An Historical Overview of Black Museums
and Institutions with Museums Functions, 1800-1980."  Negro History
Bulletin, 44:56-58 (July, August, September, 1981).

The author analyzes the important role played by churches,
benevolent societies, library groups and expositions in the Afro-
American community's search for self-identity and in its attempt to
preserve its heritage.  The author traces the history and need for
black museums and cultural institutions in a racist society, from
their early beginnings in churches and school fairs to the
establishment of museums in black institutions such as Howard and
Wilberforce Universities, the establishment of separate black
expositions following Plessy v. Ferguson, the founding of the
Association for the Study of Afro-American Life and History and the
Harlem renaissance.

324.  Dann, Martin E., ed.  The Black Press, 1827-1890:  The Quest for
National Identity.  New York:  G. P. Putnam's, Sons, 1971.

A collection of articles from numerous black newspapers, the work
provides a useful starting point for the scholar investigating the
educating influence of the black press in the nineteenth-century
black community, both before and after the Civil War.  The black
press promoted self-help, moral uplift, education, the establishment of libraries, reading rooms and lectures.  After the Civil War,
the black press also emphasized racial pride, and called for the
uplifting and educating of the black female.

325.  Daniel, Walter G., and John B. Holden.  Ambrose Caliver:  Adult
Educator and Civil Servant.  Washington, D.C.:  The Adult Education
Association of the USA, 1966.

This monograph focuses on the professional life of Ambrose Caliver
(1894-1962).  Caliver, a black man, is recognized by adult education
scholars as a mentor in the field, noted for his devotion to adult
education for all races.  He was elected president of the Adult
Education Association of the U.S.A. in 1961.

326.  David, Jay, and Elaine Crane.  The Black Soldier.  New York:
William Morrow and Co., 1971.

The authors provide an implicit account of the vital part education
played in a Negro soldier's life.

327.  Davie, Maurice R.  Negroes in American Society.  New York:
McGraw-Hill, 1949.

One chapter is devoted to a discussion of Negro education both
before and after the Civil War.  Davie argues that educational
opportunities for Negroes prior to the Civil War were restricted
primarily to the North.

328.  Davis, Lenwood G.  The Black Aged in the United States.  Westport,
Conn.:  Greenwood Press, 1980.

This book is an annotated bibliography on works dealing with the
black aged in the United States.  The resources annotated include
articles, books, monographs, dissertations, theses and government
publications.

329.  DuBois, W. E. B.  Atlanta Universities Publication, Vol. II,
No. 7-11, 1902-1906.  New York:  Octagon Books, 1968 reprint. No. 7
The Negro Artisan (1902).

DuBois provides a description and critical analysis of the Negro
artisan both before and after the Civil War.  Much of the focus
is on describing the trades themselves rather than on the training
received.  DuBois lists five weaknesses often associated with
industrial training itself:  the high cost, lack of distinction
between training teachers who may teach industrial subjects and
trades training for artisans, undue emphasis upon the practical,
tendency to ignore changing conditions in the industrial world and
graduating only a small number of artisans.

330.  Fenderson, Lewis H.  "The Negro Press as a Social Instrument."
Journal of Negro Education, 20:181-188 (Spring, 1951).

Beginning primarily as a protest institution, the black press
expanded its functions to include:  (1) dissemination of Negro
news, (2) cultivation of racial good will, (3) call for the
integration of the Negro into the mainstream pattern of American
society and (4) replying to vindictive articles in the white press.
Fenderson's article serves as a useful study of the influence of
the black press in educating the black community on the importance of
moving toward a fuller integration within American Society.

331.  Foner, Philip S., and Ronald L. Lewis.  The Black Worker:  A
Documentary History From Colonial Times to the Present, Vol. I, The
Black Worker to 1869.  Philadelphia:  Temple University Press,
1978.

This work contains a collection of primary source materials
encompassing the history of the Afro-American laborer in both the
North and the South, focusing on the artisan, mechanic and
craftsman but excluding the laborer in the agricultural sector.
Although the collection focuses primarily on working conditions and
employment of blacks it does include references to education,
especially in the documents dealing with the apprenticeship system
and in the documents demonstrating skills learned by the black
laborer.

332.  Franklin, Vincent P.  The Education of Black Philadelphia.
Philadelphia:  University of Pennsylvania Press, 1979.

Franklin describes and analyzes the activities of individuals and groups in promoting education for black Philadelphians. One such individual was the Quaker, Anthony Benezet, who took the lead in providing academic and manual training to slaves and ex-slaves during the Colonial era. Important group activities included the lecture series on black heritage sponsored by the American Negro Historical Society, the educational activities of the YMCA, NAACP, black sororities and fraternities, black civic organizations and the efforts of the Colored Women's Society to improve the social and recreational conditions of blacks in the city of Philadelphia. Also noted are numerous all-black evening classes in basic literacy training in the 1920's sponsored by the Philadelphia Board of Public Education.

333. _____, and James D. Anderson, eds.  New Perspectives on Black Educational History. Boston:  G. K. Hall & Co., 1978.

This book is a collection of essays which grew out of the sixty-first annual convention of the Association for the Study of Afro-American Life and History, Chicago 1976. According to the editors, "this work is a reconnaissance, that is, an attempt by a group of young historians to provide a preliminary survey of current research interests and topics in Afro-American educational history in order to initiate a dialogue with other researchers in this and related fields about the education of black folks in the United States."

Of particular interest are the essays entitled "The Michigan Avenue YMCA and the Advancement of Blacks in Buffalo, New York, 1922-1940" by Lillian S. Williams and "In pursuit of Freedom:  The Educational Activities of Black Social Organizations in Philadelphia, 1900-1930" by Vincent P. Franklin.

334. Frazier, E. Franklin.  Black Bourgeoisie. Glencoe, Ill.:  The Free Press, 1957.

The roots of the black bourgeoisie in America extend back to the free Negro prior to the Civil War. Although many free blacks were able to amass considerable wealth prior to Emancipation, the modern business practices of the Negro elite really did not take hold until the close of the War.

Free blacks were considerably better off than those of their race who were disenfranchised. The author reports on the educational activities of the black bourgeoisie.

335. _____.  The Negro in the United States. New York: MacMillan, 1949.

Franklin provides a comprehensive history of the American Negro, from the arrival of the first Africans on American soil to the late 1940's. Various aspects of black education are addressed.

336. Green, Constance M.  The Secret City. Princeton, N.J.:  Princeton University Press, 1967.

This book focuses on race relations in Washington, D.C., from
approximately 1791 to 1965. Education of the Negro, and all of its
ramifications, greatly impacted upon the ability of both races to
coexist as a community in the Nation's capitol city.

337. Hayden, Robert, and Eugene DuBois. "A Drum Major for Black Adult
Education: Alan L. Locke." The Western Journal of Black Studies,
1:494-496 (December, 1977).

The Afro-American that has perhaps been most influential in the
adult education movement in the United States is Alain LeRoy Locke.
Locke (1886-1954) was born into an educated family in Philadelphia,
Pennsylvania. His mother was a school teacher and his father a
lawyer. After he was graduated from Philadelphia's School of
Pedagogy, Locke entered Harvard University where he received the
A.B. Degree and was elected Phi Beta Kappa. He also received his
Ph.D. from the same institution.

He taught at Howard University for more than forty years. During
many of those years he was chairman of the Department of Philosophy.

His formal ties to the adult education movement began in 1924 when
he was asked to be a delegate to the first national convention which
resulted in the formation of the American Association for Adult
Education. Locke was elected president of this organization in
1946.

The article highlights the achievements of this Afro-American mentor
of adult education whose career in the field lasted nearly three
decades.

338. Haynes, George E. The Trend of the Races. New York: Council of
Women for Home Missions, 1922.

This book is the result of a study of the progress of the Negro from
the Civil War to the 1920's. The author credits Northern missionary
teachers for much of the educational progress that Negroes of all
ages made during this period.

339. Hogg, Thomas G. "Negroes and Their Institutions in Oregon."
Phylon, 30:272-285 (Fall, 1969).

In this historical overview of the Negro in Oregon, the author
describes provisions for educational and recreational opportunities
available to the blacks in this Western state.

340. Johnsen, Julia E. The Negro Problem. New York: H. W. Wilson
Co., 1921.

The Negro Problem is a selected collection of articles dealing with
problems of Negro Americans. In the chapter, "The Education of the
Southern Negro," Johnsen traces the history of one problem, education,
from the pre-Revolutionary era to the late nineteenth century.
Included here are the benevolent societies' efforts in educating the
Negro adult.

, Charles.  "The Rise of the Negro Magazine."  Journal of
, 13:7-21 (January, 1928).

ant vehicle for the education of the black community was
magazine, notwithstanding its middle- and upper-class
bias.  Johnson traces the seven "stages" of the Negro magazine from
the pre-Civil War period to the early twentieth century and analyzes
the magazine's purpose at each stage.

342.  Kelsey, Lincoln D.  Cooperative Extension Work.  Ithaca, N.Y.:
Comstock Publishing Associates, 1963.

This is a treatise on the Cooperative Extension Program created by
the Smith-Lever Act of 1914.  The program stimulated American adult
education by providing instruction in many aspects of agriculture
and home economics.  Black adults have, however, been recipients of
this valuable training only on a limited basis.

343.  Knowles, Malcolm S.  A History of the Adult Education Movement in
the United States.  Huntington, N.Y.:  Robert E. Krieger Pub., Co., 1977.

A standard history of American Adult Education, it is written
primarily from the practitioner's point of view.  Its strength is in
cataloging the different types of adult education programs in a
chronological sequence.  Its major weakness, however, is its failure
to adequately critique adult education programs from a critical
public policy perspective analyzing program outcomes in terms of
class and race.  This is especially evident in the discussion of
black adult education which is conspicious by its nearly total
ommission.  Except for several comments relative to educational
programs sponsored by the NAACP and the Urban League in the early
twentieth century and Knowles' indictment of governmental policy
in the Reconstruction era, especially for its failure to use adult
education as an instrument of national policy for the freedmen, one
would never suspect that adult education had had any place in
Afro-American history.

344.  Lerner, Gerda, ed.  Black Women in White America:  A Documentary
History.  New York:  Pantheon Books--Random House, 1972.

Lerner's documentary contains several brief but relevant sections
for the study of black adult education.  One is the section on
teaching the freedmen.  Of special note here is Susie King Taylor's
reminiscences entitled, "A Former Slave Teaches Black Soldiers."
The other is the section on benevolent societies and the national
club movement containing selections on the origin and educational
activities of selected clubs.

345.  Levine, Lawrence.  Black Culture and Black Consciousness:  Afro-
American Folk Thought from Slavery to Freedom.  New York:  Oxford
University Press, 1977.

A provocative study based on sound judgment and thorough research,
Levine's history of Afro-American folk thought is indispensible for
the study of educational experiences of the black community.  Two
topics are of special interest for the study of the education of the

black adult. One is Levine's study of the sacred and oral world of the slave, highlighting the importance of slave music, slave religion and slave folk belief in creating "the necessary space between the slaves and their owners," thereby preventing legal slavery from becoming complete spiritual or cultural slavery. The second topic is Levine's analysis of the impact of literacy upon the blacks' perception and world view.

Levine's focus is on what blacks believed and on how they perceived the world, rather than on what whites thought they should believe. He concludes that the slave community was successful in maintaining its culture, its heritage was not totally erased through the severity of slavery. Cultural fusion was not merely a one-way street, white culture was influenced by Afro-American culture as well.

346. Mabe, Carleton. Black Education in New York State: From Colonial to Modern Times. Syracuse, N.Y.: Syracuse University Press, 1979.

Although much of the book deals with the education of black children and youth, chapters 1 and 3 contain useful material for the study of black adult education as well. Chapter 1 focuses on education for slaves, including the goals and activities of the Society for the Propogation of the Gospel in religious instruction and literacy training. Chapter 3 deals with the importance of the Sunday School in providing religious instruction and literacy training prior to 1861.

347. Madden, Samuel A. "Adult Education and the American Negro." Adult Education Bulletin, 5:136-139 (June, 1941).

This is an excellent concise overview of Negro adult education in America. The article identifies many of the educational programs for Negroes from the time of their arrival to 1941. The article is also insightful and the author seems to be sensitive to the Negro's cause.

348. McGee, Leo. "Decline of Black Owned Rural Land: Implications for Adult Education." Adult Leadership, 35:207-209 (March, 1977).

The year 1910 represents the peak year of black landownership in the United States. At that time it is estimated that blacks owned 15 million acres of land. Since then there has been a precipitous decline in black landownership. Some of the reasons cited for this land loss include: (1) black migration from the South to Northern and Western cities; (2) less than altruistic behavior patterns of lawyers, land speculators and county officials with respect to real estate transactions involving blacks; and, (3) widespread illiteracy among rural black adults.

Illiteracy is a major contributor to black land decline. Due to the lack of educational skills, black landowners have been unable to: (1) transform their rural acreage into a viable investment; (2) write wills; (3) intelligently negotiate real estate contracts; and, (4) understand the specifics of property taxes, mortgage foreclosures and partition sales.

The article challenges officials responsible for adult education programming to assist in the improvement of the educational level of disadvantaged blacks, particularly those in rural communities. In this way, instant laboratories can be created for students in graduate programs in adult education to broaden their experience while providing humanitarian service to less fortunate. Concerned, progressive adult educators can ill-afford to allow the depletion of the largest black equity base in the South to continue due to the lack of educational skills.

349. _____. "A Study of Black Rural Land Ownership and Control: Problems and Attitudes of Black Adults Concerning Rural Land in Tennessee." The Tennessee Adult Educator, 11:6-12 (Winter, 1978).

This was a two-year study funded by the U.S. Department of Agriculture. The research sample consisted of 147 black rural landowners in three counties. The study was undertaken to yield information on the status and trends of black landownership, provide information with regard to institutional practices associated with land transfers and determine the attitudes held by blacks toward rural land in Tennessee.

In the findings of the study, it is reiterated that illiteracy among blacks is a major cause of rural land loss. Many other interesting findings are presented in this treatise.

350. McGinnis, Frederick A. The Education of Negroes in Ohio. Blanchester, Ohio: Curless Printing Company, 1962.

The author discusses the obstacles to and efforts in educating Ohio Negroes. He highlights the efforts of the American Colonization Society, supported by such influential members as Thomas Jefferson, James Madison, Daniel Webster, Henry Clay and Bushrod Washington-- the latter a nephew of George Washington and a justice of the Supreme Court--in blocking the education of black Americans. In contrast, the black churches, most noteably the African Methodist Church, took the lead in providing educational opportunities for blacks of all ages.

351. Meier, August. "The Beginning of Industrial Education in Negro Schools." The Midwest Journal, 7:21-44 (Spring, 1955).

Meier traces the industrial education movement for blacks from the pre-Civil War era to the rise of Hampton and Tuskegee Institutes. He points out that industrial training was promoted by the Negro Convention of 1853 and that many of Samuel Armstrong's and Booker T. Washington's arguments were already enunciated by Frederick Douglas.

352. Muraskin, William. "The Hidden Role of Fraternal Organizations in the Education of Black Adults: Prince Hall Freemasonry As a Case Study." Adult Education, 26:235-252 (1976).

One multi-faceted institution not normally associated with learning is the Prince Hall Freemasonry, the black branch of the international Freemasonic Order. Begun in 1775, it is the oldest and most prestigious black fraternal order. Most of its members occupy middle-class status within black society and its membership numbers in the hundreds of thousands.

The Fraternity has been most successful in teaching manners, social graces, intellectual and practical business skills, citizenship training and moral codes. This article discusses the educational role of the Fraternity during the last 200 years.

353. Mydrall, Gunnar. _An American Dilemma_. New York: Harper and Brothers, 1944.

"The education of Negroes under slavery cannot be discussed without noting the excellent training as artisans and handicraftsmen a small portion of slaves received. Each plantation was a more or less self-sufficient economy outside of its major crop export and food import, and, therefore, required slaves with each of the skills necessary to keep up the community."

This 1,483 page book covers numerous aspects of the Negro experience in America. Many are directly or indirectly related to adult education.

354. Reid, Ira De A. _Adult Education Among Negroes_. Washington, D.C.: The Associates in Negro Folk Education, 1936.

This is generally considered the first book-length work on the subject of "Negro Adult Education." Reid was Professor of Sociology at Atlanta University when he completed this treatise. His primary goal was to make the American public aware of the special educational needs of this country's black adult population.

This seventy-three page book covers four areas: Historical perspective of adult education in Denmark, which is considered by many to have had the first organized program in adult education, and the United States; adult education programs for Negroes in the U.S.; plan for organizing adult education programs in a given community; and, an annotated bibliography.

355. Reuter, Edward B. _The American Race Problem_. New York: Thomas Y. Crowell Co., 1966.

Chapter 13 entitled, "The Education of the Negro," includes an extensive history of Negro Education from the Colonial era to the twentieth century.

356. Romero, Patricia. _International Library of Negro Life and History--I too am America_. New York: Publishers Co., Inc., 1968.

This pictorial publication includes a section dealing with the _Freedman's Journal_ which was the first newspaper in the United States to be owned and printed by blacks. This adult education medium was published by John B. Russwurm and Samuel E. Cornish and was first released in 1927.

357.  Rose, Arnold.  The Negro in America.  New York:  Harper and
Brothers, 1944.

> This book includes a chapter entitled "Church, School and Press" in
> which the author indirectly shows how these topics are related to
> the education of the black adult.

358.  Shim Kin, Demitri B.  The Extended Family in Black Societies.
Chicago:  Mouton Publishers, 1978.

> This work consists of essays on the Black Extended Family.  Negro
> adult education is briefly referenced.

359.  Thompson, Daniel C.  Sociology of the Black Experience.  Westport,
Conn.:  Greenwood Press, 1974.

> Chapter 6, "Education," is summed up in the first paragraph:
>
> "The Blacks' struggle to acquire a 'good' education has been long,
> frustrating, and dangerous.  Motivating the struggle has been the
> conviction that education is the key to individual dignity, social
> status, and equal citizenship.  Even during the slave period when
> the education of Blacks was prohibited by law and when those who
> violated that law were severely punished, many slaves dared to
> attend 'clandestine' schools and learned to read and write whenever
> and however they could manage to do so."

360.  Thorpe, Earl E.  The Mind of the Negro:  An Intellectual History
of Afro Americans.  Baton Rouge, La.:  Ortlieb Press, 1961.

> Chapter 14 is entitled "Elements of Negro Thought on Education and
> Segregation."  In this section the author points out that many
> decades before emancipation free Negroes as well as the enslaved put
> a high premium on education.  Education was perhaps considered the
> most powerful tool in their fight for freedom and equality.

361.  True, Alfred C.  A History of Agricultural Extension Work in the
United States, 1785-1923.  Washington, D.C.:  Government Printing Office,
1928.

> The author points out that agricultural extension in this country had
> its beginning around the 1780's.  It initiated the most massive adult
> education effort ever attempted in America, providing education
> services to the farmer, the homemaker and the general public.  During
> the initial years and extending to some degree to today, one of the
> major projects has been the Negro Ministers' Institute.

362.  Weatherford, W. D.  Negro Life in the South.  New York:  YMCA
Press, 1910.

> In the chapter, "Education of the Negro," Weatherford discusses the
> education of the Negro from slavery through the Freedmen's Bureau era.

363.  Wesley, Charles H.  International Library of Negro Life and
History--The Quest for Equality.  New York:  Publishers Co., Inc., 1968.

This pictorial work devotes some attention to the organization and educational contribution of the Negro Church. From Colonial times to the present, the church has been a valuable resource to the black community.

364. _____ . Negro Labor in the United States, 1850-1925: A Study in American Economic History. New York: Vanguard Press, 1927.

Wesley surveys the conditions of black labor from the period of slavery to the "entrance of negroes (sic) into industrial occupations." Although the focus is primarily on the occupations rather than on education, several sections include material directly relevant for a study of black education, including adult education. Included are discussions on organized groups of "Colored Laborers" in the antebellum, Northern cities promoting education, including manual training, for upward mobility; the Industrial School Movement of the 1870's and 1880's; and, the Conference of Farmers at Tuskegee and its promotion of scientific agriculture. Wesley provides a sympathetic and positive evaluation of the work at Hampton and Tuskegee Institutes, arguing that their emphasis in industrial training was made necessary by the discriminatory practices of trade unions in excluding blacks from apprenticeship programs.

365. West, Earle H. A Bibliography of Doctoral Research on the Negro 1933-1966. Ann Arbor: University Microfilms, 1969.

The bibliography contains listings of doctoral research on the Negro during the period 1933-1966. The 1,452 listings cover various aspects of study relating to the Negro in the United States and are arranged in seven categories--Social Institutions and Conditions, Individual Characteristics, Economic Status and Problems, Education, History, Political and Civil Rights and Humanities.

366. Williams, George W. History of the Negro Race in America, 1619-1880. New York: Putnam's Son, 1883.

This comprehensive volume explores in detail nearly every aspect of the Negro experience in America and, to some extent, his existence prior to arrival from the mother country. Education makes up an integral part of the content.

367. Wilson, Joseph T. The Black Phalanx: A History of the Negro Soldiers in the United States in the Wars of 1775, 1812, 1861-1865. Hartford, Conn.: American Publishing Co., 1890.

The Negro played a significant role in the Wars of 1775, 1812 and the Civil War. Of all the wars, the most concerted effort to educate the Negro soldier was made during the Civil War. He received instruction in the rudiments of education from military chaplains, military officers and their wives and military officers and civilians of his own race. The War itself was an educational experience for the 200,000 men of African descent who enlisted. This book may well be the first to give an account of Negro participation in these major wars and the implications of what they meant to him educationally.

# AUTHOR INDEX

# SUBJECT INDEX

## About the Authors

LEO McGEE is Assistant Dean of Extended Services and Professor of Education at Tennessee Technological University. He is the co-author of *The Black Rural Landowner: Endangered Species* (Greenwood Press, 1979) as well as a contributor to *Journal of Negro Education, Black Scholar, Adult Leadership*, and *Journal of Lifelong Learning*.

HARVEY G. NEUFELDT is a Professor in the Department of Secondary Education and Foundations at Tennessee Technological University. He has contributed chapters to *Education and the Rise of the New South* and *Religion and Morality in American Schooling* and has published articles in the *Review Journal of Philosophy and Social Science, Educational Studies*, and *Journal of Thought*.